THE BEDFORD SERIES IN HISTORY AND CULTURE

The Silk Roads

A Brief History with Documents

Related Titles in
THE BEDFORD SERIES IN HISTORY AND CULTURE
Advisory Editors: Lynn Hunt, *University of California, Los Angeles*
David W. Blight, *Yale University*
Bonnie G. Smith, *Rutgers University*
Natalie Zemon Davis, *Princeton University*
Ernest R. May, *Harvard University*

THE BEDFORD SERIES IN HISTORY AND CULTURE

The Silk Roads
A Brief History with Documents

Xinru Liu
The College of New Jersey

BEDFORD / ST. MARTIN'S   Boston ◆ New York

For Bedford/St. Martin's

Publisher for History: Mary V. Dougherty
Executive Editor for History: Traci M. Crowell
Director of Development for History: Jane Knetzger
Senior Editor: Heidi L. Hood
Developmental Editor: Ann Hofstra Grogg
Production Supervisor: Lisa Chow
Executive Marketing Manager: Jenna Bookin Barry
Associate Editor: Jennifer Jovin
Editorial Assistant: Laura Kintz
Project Management: Books By Design, Inc.
Cartography: Mapping Specialists, Ltd.
Text Designer: Claire Seng-Niemoeller
Cover Designer: Marine Miller
Cover Art: From the Collection of the Fujita Museum, Osaka, Japan. First section, tenth chapter of the painted scroll, *Genjo sanzo e* (Japanese National Treasure).
Composition: Achorn International, Inc.
Printing and Binding: LSC Communications, Inc.

President: Joan E. Feinberg
Editorial Director: Denise B. Wydra
Director of Marketing: Karen R. Soeltz
Director of Production: Susan W. Brown
Associate Director, Editorial Production: Elise S. Kaiser
Manager, Publishing Services: Andrea Cava

Library of Congress Control Number: 2012930087

For information, write: Bedford/St. Martin's, 75 Arlington Street, Boston, MA 02116 (617-399-4000)

ISBN: 978-0-312-47551-2

Acknowledgments
Acknowledgments and copyrights are continued at the back of the book on pages 180–81, which constitute an extension of the copyright page.

Distributed outside North America by PALGRAVE MACMILLAN
Houndmills, Basingstoke, Hampshire RG21 6XS

Foreword

The Bedford Series in History and Culture is designed so that readers can study the past as historians do.

The historian's first task is finding the evidence. Documents, letters, memoirs, interviews, pictures, movies, novels, or poems can provide facts and clues. Then the historian questions and compares the sources. There is more to do than in a courtroom, for hearsay evidence is welcome, and the historian is usually looking for answers beyond act and motive. Different views of an event may be as important as a single verdict. How a story is told may yield as much information as what it says.

Along the way the historian seeks help from other historians and perhaps from specialists in other disciplines. Finally, it is time to write, to decide on an interpretation and how to arrange the evidence for readers.

Each book in this series contains an important historical document or group of documents, each document a witness from the past and open to interpretation in different ways. The documents are combined with some element of historical narrative — an introduction or a biographical essay, for example — that provides students with an analysis of the primary source material and important background information about the world in which it was produced.

Each book in the series focuses on a specific topic within a specific historical period. Each provides a basis for lively thought and discussion about several aspects of the topic and the historian's role. Each is short enough (and inexpensive enough) to be a reasonable one-week assignment in a college course. Whether as classroom or personal reading, each book in the series provides firsthand experience of the challenge — and fun — of discovering, recreating, and interpreting the past.

Lynn Hunt
David W. Blight
Bonnie G. Smith
Natalie Zemon Davis
Ernest R. May

Exchange of jade and silk is better than of swords in a battlefield.

—Old Chinese proverb

Preface

The Silk Roads have captured the popular imagination in recent decades. Today, anything that relates to these ancient trade routes becomes a tourist attraction, drawing people to both museums in cosmopolitan areas and the caravan tracks of Central Asia. Academic study of the Silk Roads first began more than a century ago through the work of archaeologists and art historians. With the discovery of inscriptions, coins, and manuscripts at sites on the various Central Asian routes, philologists and epigraphers, including numismatists, joined the enterprise. For historians, this trade network is fascinating not only for the exchange of silks and other luxuries but especially for the exchange of ideas that it facilitated. Religions, cultural values, technologies, and imperial strategies traveled the Silk Roads, influencing and enriching civilizations from China to the Mediterranean Sea.

Students in world history classes will benefit from a synthesis. They need an overview of the growth and development of trade in the context of the millennium-long rise and fall of empires across three continents. At the same time, to appreciate the complexity and sophistication of networks of material and cultural exchange in the premodern world, they need to hear the voices of real people who lived during these centuries. With this volume I have sought both to provide an overview and to make available to students the primary sources that I use to teach and write about the Silk Roads.

The Silk Roads: A Brief History with Documents begins with an introduction that presents a narrative outline of historical developments. It highlights the expansion of trade, the diffusion of religions, the transfer of technologies, and the course of migrations and imperial conquests. The thirty-four documents that follow come from cultures ranging from China to the Mediterranean world. They date from the second century BCE, when envoys and traders from the Han Empire of China first ventured into Central Asia, to the thirteenth century CE, when the volume of maritime trade surpassed trade along the old land routes. They were written by court historians, scholars, traders, officials, soldiers, sailors, housewives, and religious teachers and pilgrims, many of whom left neither names nor identities. The documents are arranged in a roughly chronological order, but also by region and empire, to make the vast array comprehensible. Document headnotes give background on the individuals who created them, when known, and establish their context. Foreign terms and specific references are explained in footnotes.

A chronology details the rise and fall of empires along the Silk Roads and other notable events. For classroom use, questions for consideration prompt students to make connections among the documents — and thus among the cultures represented. An annotated selected bibliography gives suggestions for further reading. One map charts the land and sea routes of trade, and another presents the migrations and conquests of various ethnic groups across Eurasia. Several images with explanatory captions testify to the cultural, religious, and linguistic transmissions of Silk Roads exchanges. These aids will, I hope, help students grasp the large picture and discern the subtleties of Silk Roads history.

A NOTE ABOUT THE TEXT

The principal challenge of collecting documents related to the Silk Roads is that they exist in so many different languages and scripts. Whenever English translations were available, which was the case for many of the documents from China, the Roman Empire, and the Abbasid Caliphate, I used them, taking advantage of work by scholars well-versed in these languages and cultures. Documents excavated from Central Asian sites are often fragmentary and difficult to decipher. For example, a document in the Kharoshthi script recording one of several Central Asian dialects may contain many words from other languages or dialects. Thus the translations done by even the best of scholars may not be perfect, but they do indicate the multicultural nature of the societies located on the Silk Roads.

Remarkably, when I started this project, none of the Chinese inscriptions and manuscripts found in Turfan, Dunhuang, and the watchtowers along the Great Wall had been translated into English, so I translated them myself. These texts also present many problems. They were not meant to be literary works, and thus they were not written in classical Chinese, but instead in local vernaculars with simplified, nonstandard, and even self-invented characters. In such situations I did my best to capture the writers' meanings. In addition, peoples living along the Silk Roads used a number of terms for trade goods, as well as other things, that are not meaningful to modern readers of Chinese. I did my best to match these terms to artifacts from archaeological excavations. Above all, I aimed to reveal the thoughts and emotions of the men and women who, so long ago, left their words on wooden slips and paper.

In the introduction and my own English translations of documents, pinyin, the official system of Romanization, is applied to personal and place names. For English translations by scholars who used the Wade-Giles system, I have provided pinyin equivalents in the footnotes. To highlight topics for readers, subheads within documents are occasionally supplied; these are shown in brackets to distinguish them from subheads that are original to the documents or that indicate separate documents within groups from archaeological excavations.

ACKNOWLEDGMENTS

I am grateful to Bedford/St. Martin's for offering me the opportunity to compile a documentary textbook on the Silk Roads. This opportunity came at the invitation of Bonnie G. Smith, an eminent scholar in world history with whom I have been fortunate to collaborate. Thanks are due to Heidi Hood, senior editor at Bedford, who found the best developmental editor, Ann Hofstra Grogg, to guide me through the intricate job of editing the documents. Without her guidance I would not have seen the light at the end of the tunnel. I also wish to thank Andrea Cava at Bedford and Nancy Benjamin at Books By Design for guiding the book through production and Sybil Sosin for copyediting the manuscript. The following reviewers of earlier drafts offered helpful remarks and suggestions that made the book more comprehensible to college students: Craig Benjamin, Grand Valley State University; Steven C. Davidson, Southwestern University; Soshana Keller, Hamilton College; and Robert Strayer, California State University, Monterey Bay.

My friend and mentor Lynda Norene Shaffer generously provided guidance and constructive criticism throughout the entire process. She shares my excitement about the extraordinary information made available by these documents. Because I read neither Arabic nor Persian, I enlisted help from a well-known scholar on Islamic history, Denise Spellberg, to verify sources for the Islamic world. Furthermore, I have been very lucky to have the assistance of a young scholar from my college, Beatrice Kwok, who helped prepare the manuscript for production.

Last but not least, I must thank my husband, Dr. Weiye Li, who has always supported my work and continues to do so even during the most difficult times in his life.

Xinru Liu

Contents

Maps and Illustrations

PART ONE

Introduction:
From the Rise of the Silk
Roads to a Eurasian
Market System

The Silk Roads that carried trade goods between China and the lands of the Mediterranean for more than a millennium facilitated a multitude of cross-cultural transactions. Traders and religious pilgrims traveled these roads, spreading ideas as well as merchandise and linking peoples throughout Eurasia and many parts of Africa. Local transactions along the routes sustained communities of merchants, nomads, farmers, and monks. Commercial and cultural activities spurred political and social developments that spread across three continents. No travel corridor is more important in world history.

The term *Silk Road* is often used in a narrow sense, referring only to the land routes through Central Asia that first delivered Chinese silks to the West. This book adopts the broadest definition of the Silk Roads, presenting the formation and development of the vast commercial networks, including sea-lanes, that ultimately involved so much more than silk and encompassed much of the world.

From the second century BCE through the thirteenth century CE, peoples from Eurasia and Africa's great agricultural empires, nomadic tribes and federations, and desert oases and ports participated in the commercial transactions that took place along the Silk Roads. When the

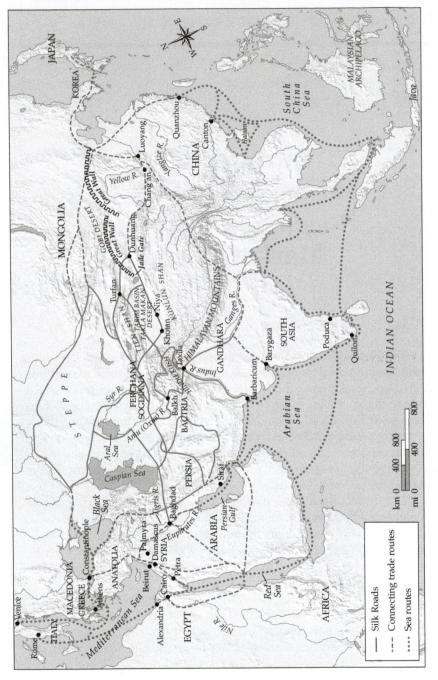

Map 1. *The Silk Roads and Sea Routes, 1–1300 CE*

Han Empire ruled China beginning in the late third century BCE, both mutually beneficial trade and imperial conflicts with the steppe nomads to the north caused great volumes of silk to flow out of China across the political and geographic divide marked by the Great Wall. By the first century CE, Chinese silk had reached the markets of the Kushan Empire in Central and South Asia, the Parthian Empire of Persia (modern Iran), and the Roman Empire based around the Mediterranean Sea. At the same time, Buddhism spread beyond India's borders, following the Silk Roads to Central Asia and China. In the early third century, when the Han and Parthian Empires were collapsing and the Roman Empire was beginning to lose its vigor, Buddhist institutions were already well established in the Silk Roads' desert oases between Central Asia and China. They were thus able to sustain the critical infrastructure on the long-distance routes and to keep trade moving during this difficult time. In the seventh century, after China reunified, its Tang Empire traded with the Sassanid Empire in Persia and the Byzantine Empire in the eastern Mediterranean. Subsequently, nomadic Turks, originally from the easternmost steppe, began to play an important role in the political and commercial relationships among empires along the Silk Roads. In addition to Buddhism, missions promoting Zoroastrianism, Manichaeism, Christianity, and Islam traveled the Silk Roads, encouraging the exchange of ideas as well as religious practices. The golden age of the overland Silk Roads began to wane at the end of the ninth century when the Tang Empire was collapsing. Although China's economy and foreign trade continued to flourish under the Song dynasty, which rose not long after the Tang fell, most goods now traveled by sea.

Interactions among the political units and social groups along the Silk Roads were not always peaceful. Nevertheless, the travelers who went to foreign lands, either for warfare or for trade, brought with them their own languages, knowledge, technologies, religions, and customs; when they returned home with new goods and trophies, they also brought back at least some new ways of doing and thinking about things. Nomadic groups that invaded and occupied agricultural lands had to impose their own languages upon the conquered people or adopt the language of their subjects in order to collect taxes and maintain order. Soldiers on the frontiers came into contact with people from many different lands and ethnicities. Traders who arrived in foreign cities sought religious institutions affiliated with their homelands to get advice about local markets. All these travelers transformed themselves at the same time that they transformed the places in which they settled. The documents in this book help us to understand the lives and thoughts of these travelers, entrepreneurs, and pilgrims of past centuries and to appreciate how they spread both goods and ideas from many lands throughout Eurasia and parts of Africa.

CHINA'S TRADE ON THE WESTERN FRONTIER, SECOND–FIRST CENTURIES BCE

China's Great Wall, a defense system built across its northern border, was essentially a stone fence that separated farmers in the agricultural zones to the south from the horseback-riding nomads to the north. When, late in the third century BCE, the founder of the Qin Empire (221–206 BCE) extended the walls of the northern states he conquered, he intended to fend off the Xiongnu nomads. The Xiongnu had a long history of hostilities with China, and their formidable force of horseback-riding archers made frequent incursions into the agricultural villages on China's northern frontier to steal grains, silk textiles, alcohol, and anything else that could not be produced on the steppe.

Silk was especially prized. As early as the Han dynasty (206 BCE–220 CE), the Chinese exported a variety of silk products. Light, translucent silk crepe was woven with very long filaments, each one harvested by carefully unraveling the single thread that makes up an entire cocoon. Most likely, at that time only Chinese women had mastered the skill of reeling up this single filament while the cocoon was still floating in boiling water. There was also a medium-weight silk material, now known as damask, that had elaborate raised patterns woven into the fabric using only a single color of thread. To make such patterns, weavers had to repeatedly change the threading on the loom. A heavy textile, now called brocade or tapestry, was woven with a variety of different colored threads; it required even more complicated looms and highly skilled workers. These types of silk were made in workshops owned by the imperial government and were intended only for the imperial family and court officials. Chinese emperors prohibited commoners, including rich merchants, from wearing silk tapestries and embroidered silk clothes. The overwhelming majority of silk textiles made in and exported from China were not these luxurious silks, however, but relatively thin silk now referred to as plain tabby. This silk was produced by Chinese farm families, who raised mulberry trees, fed their leaves to silkworms, boiled their cocoons, and unwound the cocoons to make thread. They paid their taxes to the government in grains and bolts of plain silk, which for about a thousand years also served as a kind of currency in China's economy.[1]

During these years, the emperors of agricultural China were dependent upon steppe peoples for horses, the fastest means of overland transport before the nineteenth-century steam engine. Since Chinese farmers used all available land to raise crops, they lacked the large pastures necessary for the best varieties of horses to flourish and breed. Thus the Great Wall was actually a barrier with many gates, at which markets were established. Nomads who wanted to trade their horses for grains and silk came to these markets, as did farmers with products. As long as China's imperial government was strong, the Great Wall was an efficient system for both protecting the border and facilitating trade. Due to this silk-horse trade, China's silk rapidly became famous along its northern steppe frontier as the most beautiful and comfortable textile. Within a century of the construction of the Great Wall, silk's reputation and market had spread throughout much of Eurasia and North Africa.

The founder of the Qin Empire could not purchase horses from the Xiongnu, his fiercest adversary on the steppe. Instead, he bought horses from another nomadic people, the Yuezhi, who seasonally moved their herds and their homes in the northern foothills of the Tien Shan—the Heavenly Mountains—a Central Asian range now within China's Xinjiang Uighur Autonomous Region. The Yuezhi sold better horses than the Xiongnu, in part because they had better grasslands and better breeds; they were also sellers of jade, a precious stone found in the Kunlun Mountains. They sold these items to the Qin Empire for silks, which they then sold to other nomads, garnering great profits. Yuezhi horses helped the Qin in their battles against the Xiongnu, who despised this cooperation between their chief rival on the steppe and their archenemy, China.

The Qin Empire was short-lived, and the civil wars that ensued in China provided plenty of opportunities for the Xiongnu to plunder Chinese farms. After the Han dynasty established another central government, Han emperors still found it hard to defend their northern border, even with the Great Wall (Document 1). The first few Han emperors had to marry some of their royal princesses to Xiongnu chiefs and to provide large dowries of silks, grains, and alcohol to buy peace on this border. This form of exchange, though rather one-sided, continued to deliver silks from China to the steppe.

After the Han Empire had become stronger economically and militarily, the emperor Wudi (r. 140–87 BCE) took the offensive against the Xiongnu. He sent military expeditions to chase the invaders away from the Great Wall, and he also sought allies on the steppe. Believing that the Yuezhi people who had previously traded with the Qin emperor might be allies, in 139 BCE he sent an envoy, Zhang Qian, out onto the steppe to look for them. But Zhang Qian had to pass through Xiongnu territory before reaching the Yuezhi in Bactria, a Central Asian land to which they had retreated. When in 126 BCE he finally made his way back to Chang'an, the Han capital, he was immediately recognized by officialdom as the expert on the "Western Regions." He reported everything he had learned about the nomads on the steppe, the agricultural settlements on the edges of the Takla Makan Desert, and the markets of Bactria. He even provided some information about India, which he had most likely gathered from traders in Bactria. The wonders and curiosities of the Western Regions that he described, especially the "heavenly horses," engaged the attention of the emperor, who determined to build trading networks that could bring these wonders to China (Document 2).

By this time the Xiongnu were no longer a military threat on China's northern border, but rather a rival on the trade routes linking China to the Western Regions. To secure an important part of the route along China's northwestern frontier, Wudi had the Great Wall extended westward along the Hexi Corridor, a narrow strip of land south of the Gobi Desert and north of the Qilian Mountains. The westernmost gate on the Great Wall's new extension was called Yumen,[2] literally the "Jade Gate," and thereafter it was through this gate that jade from the Western Regions was transported to the Chinese interior.

This new, more western frontier was effective in protecting traders traveling with their goods, but it was also very expensive to maintain. Supplying food to the soldiers who guarded the watchtowers along the Great Wall was a major challenge to the state granary and transportation systems. Wudi thus decreed that these soldiers could, with government help, produce their own food in this arid area. They were encouraged to bring their wives and children to the frontier and settle there. They were also given seeds, tools, and technological guidance for growing crops on what had previously been wasteland, a project that required building irrigation systems (Document 3). In addition to the food they produced, they received salaries paid in bolts of plain silk, which they could exchange for goods from the nomads or local farmers.

The success of these agricultural endeavors along the Great Wall encouraged the Han Empire to establish additional settlements of soldiers outside the Jade Gate in the Tarim Basin. There small farming oases were situated on the edges of the Takla Makan Desert where snowmelt from the Tien Shan and Kunlun Mountains provided water for agriculture. Once the silk trade began, the Han Empire protected the routes that went through the desert and encouraged agricultural development through irrigation. These programs increased the productivity of the oases, encouraging more people, including nomads, to settle there. By the end of the second century CE, as the Han Empire was collapsing, there was a well-established network of trade routes that linked the oasis towns of the Tarim Basin together. By this time, traders were transporting silks from China to Sogdiana, a land of oases east of the Amu (ancient Oxus) River, as well as to locations even farther west. Moving from the west to the east, from Central Asian oases, India, Persia, and even the Roman Empire, considerable quantities of horses, cotton cloth, woolen textiles, and glassware were flowing into Chang'an, Luoyang (another Han capital), and other major cities in China.

ROME'S TRADE TO THE EAST, FIRST CENTURY BCE–SECOND CENTURY CE

By the first century CE, the Roman Empire was the westernmost market for China's silks, and its merchants and rulers had turned their attention to the east. This was not the first time a Mediterranean empire had looked eastward. In the late fourth century BCE, the military expeditions of Alexander the Great of Macedonia had gone into Central Asia and as far east as India, and his efforts to conquer these territories brought Greek-speaking populations to many eastern lands, thereby paving the way for the easterly trade of the Roman Empire. On his way east, Alexander had allied with and recruited mercenaries from many different peoples (Document 5). Asian Scythians, for example, were horseback-riding archers who defeated a troop of Macedonians in the region of the Don (Greek Tanais) River. In revenge, Alexander massacred local peoples suspected of supporting the Scythians, but the real culprits retreated out of sight, as nomads often did. In contrast, the European Scythians, who moved their herds through the grasslands around the Black Sea, offered their services and even a princess to Alexander, though the offer was turned down. Alexander set up fortified towns from the eastern shore of the Mediterranean all the way to Bactria and Sogdiana in Central Asia, and he staffed them with Greek soldiers. These soldiers, and others who were not Greek but had been recruited on the way to India, settled in these towns and became farmers, planting vineyards and wheat fields.

Residents of these Hellenistic towns were often bilingual, using Greek for commercial and official purposes, and they maintained city-states with Greek-style institutions such as temples, theaters, and gymnasiums (Document 4). After the arrival of the Yuezhi in Bactria in the latter part of the second century BCE, these Greek-speaking cities began participating in the silk trade, and Chinese silk began flowing westward toward the Mediterranean. The Greeks had heard about silk. The Greek name for China was *Seres*, a word that was apparently derived from *si*, the Chinese word for "silk."

As the Romans gained prominence in the Mediterranean, they received tribute and trade from many lands. Women from wealthy Roman families became so enamored of silk crepe, a translucent light textile revealing their beautiful figures, that Pliny the Elder, a noted scholar, complained that the love of such oriental luxuries was draining the imperial treasury (Document 6). Pliny certainly exaggerated the financial consequences of silk importation, especially since men still wore wool dyed purple to demonstrate their status. However, once artisans began dyeing imported silks with this rare purple, silk became even more expensive and prestigious.

Roman scholars such as Pliny studied Greek documents and the writings of Greek authors to advance their knowledge of eastern lands. Nevertheless, Roman knowledge of more distant countries, such as India and China, was still limited and vague. Geographers attempting to place the names of these countries on their maps often put them in the wrong locations (Documents 5, 8), and Pliny's accounts of the origins of silk, cotton, and gemstones and of how they were produced were full of errors (Document 6). In contrast, his knowledge of the much-coveted purple dye, which came from a particular kind of shellfish of the eastern Mediterranean, was accurate. During Pliny's lifetime the Mediterranean market for silk was well-established, and his detailed descriptions of the finished goods from India and China reveal that the Romans loved luxuries and were willing to pay high prices for them. Gemstones, silks, and other fabrics dyed purple were important symbols of social status. In Rome's highly stratified society, the wealthy purchased goods that were rare, beautiful, and from faraway countries to distinguish themselves from the general population.

Both the Han and Roman Empires sought to extend their interests far beyond their territorial borders. While China protected its trade with the Western Regions by extending the Great Wall westward and supervising the coming and going of traders through the Jade Gate, the Roman Empire managed its trade with the East from the port of Alexandria on the Nile Delta. The lighthouse at Alexandria, built by Egypt's Ptolemaic regime, became the symbol of Rome's gate to its easternmost trade. Alexandria was not only the most important port on the Mediterranean, but also the one that gave access to the Arabian Sea via the Nile and a short portage across the desert to the Red Sea. The traders who set out from the port of Alexandria were Greek-speaking Egyptians, and those who traded on the overland routes that went east through the Parthian Empire were Greek-speaking Arabs. These Roman Empire traders could reach Bactria and Sogdiana by land, or they could sail from ports on the Red Sea to ports along India's western coast. Regardless of the route they took, they encountered traders from Hellenistic cities who spoke enough Greek to communicate about the quality of the goods and to bargain about the prices.

Goods from South and East Asia also came by overland routes handled by merchants based in the caravan cities of present-day Syria and Jordan, where the "Incense Road" had long enticed Mediterranean powers to trade eastward. Here Nabataeans, who spoke a variety of Arabic, built caravan cities such as Petra, where the architecture still reflects Greek styles. They, too, adopted Greek as a commercial language. Traders from these caravan cities brought spices and aromatic tree resins used as incense from the southern part of the Arabian Peninsula (present-day Yemen and Oman), where the Sabaeans, a people who spoke a dialect of Arabic, made great fortunes from frankincense and myrrh. Their ancestors had appeared in the biblical record when the queen called Sheba visited King Solomon of Israel. The Sabaeans were also a seafaring people who sailed across the Arabian Sea to purchase tropical spices such as cinnamon and pepper in Indian ports. They knew how to take advantage of the monsoons, the seasonal winds that blow across the Arabian Sea, and thus their ships could make a round trip to India within one year (Document 7).

Greek-speaking Roman traders also learned about the trade monsoons on the Arabian Sea, and they sailed from Red Sea ports to buy silk, gemstones, and spices from India. In exchange, they carried cargoes of Mediterranean wine and glassware, as well as gold and silver coins to help pay for all the items they wanted to bring back from India. They also discovered that they could make larger profits by first stopping at ports along the southern Arabian coast and trading some of their Mediterranean goods for frankincense and myrrh before heading to India, since there was a great demand in Indian markets for these famous tree resins. At this time, India's major commercial ports were Barbaricum, at the mouth of the Indus River, and Barygaza, on the Gulf of Cambay.

There Roman traders found old coins that had been issued by Hellenistic authorities in previous centuries, as well as more current coins that were inscribed with Greek letters and shared the same standard as the Roman denarii. Roman sailors explored many ports along the west coast of the Indian subcontinent and even rounded the tip to reach the east coast via the strait between the subcontinent and modern Sri Lanka. They set up a trading depot at Poduca, near modern Pondicherry, and employed both Mediterranean and local laborers to process the goods before sailing them back home. Their entrepreneurship brought a variety of luxuries, in addition to silk and pepper, to the marketplaces of the Roman Empire.[3] Thus, what had begun in China as direct exchange of silk for horses had become, by the end of the second century CE, a vast trading network in luxury goods that shaped and enriched the lives of the elite throughout Asia, Africa, and the Mediterranean world.

THE KUSHAN EMPIRE AND THE INFLUENCE OF BUDDHISM, SECOND CENTURY BCE–SECOND CENTURY CE

On both land routes and sea-lanes, traders from the West and the East encountered each other as they passed through the lands of the Kushan Empire during the first centuries CE. The empire had been built by the Yuezhi after the Xiongnu had forced them from their original homeland on the steppe just west of China. When they first arrived at the bank of the Amu River, where the Han envoy Zhang Qian eventually caught up with them, they were still very much nomads. All the adult men, who numbered between ten thousand and twenty thousand, were horseback-riding archers.[4] As agents of the silk trade, they became rich, for they possessed many good horses as well as much gold.[5] Bactria, their new home, was a fertile agricultural land, and they settled in its Hellenistic cities with Greek-style institutions and architecture. But the Yuezhi lacked experience in ruling and taxing a sedentary society. They had to learn to read and write and to keep accounts. They soon began to cast Greek-style coins with the image of the king on one side and that of a deity on the other. Their gold, silver, and copper currencies facilitated domestic and long-distance trade in both inexpensive wares and expensive luxuries.

In 50 CE, after they had been ruling Bactria for some 170 years, the Kushans crossed the Hindu Kush Mountains and invaded India. Now stronger and richer than when they left the steppe, they had profited from the wealth of an agricultural society and had an excellent cavalry. Their territory in northern India, both in the Indus River Valley and in the western part of the Ganges River Valley, was even richer than Bactria, but also more complicated to rule. Before the coming of the nomads, northwestern India, especially the region then called Gandhara (modern Pakistan and eastern Afghanistan), had been ruled by Alexander's garrisons and their descendants. These Hellenistic cities had more Indian than Greek residents but maintained the political structure of Greek city-states. Like residents of the Hellenistic cities in Asia, they had never insisted on a single religion but welcomed the worship of both local and foreign deities. The Kushans inherited this cosmopolitan tradition and patronized all the religions of the region. In fact, the Kushan kings' patronage of religious institutions was an integral part of their strategy for ruling the lands they controlled. Of the religions that prevailed in their territories at this time, Buddhism was among the most influential.

Buddhism had changed greatly since the Buddha had lived and preached in the Ganges River Valley around the fifth century BCE. When the Buddha was alive, he was respected as the wise man of the Shakya people, a small chiefdom in the foothills of the Himalayas, but not thought of as a god. For several hundred years after his death (nirvana), there were no statues of the Buddha for his followers to worship. Buddhist stupas, or shrines, might preserve relics of the Buddha amid sculptures of elephants, monkeys, and minor deities associated with nature, often represented by young maidens. A pair of footprints might represent the presence of the Buddha, and a *bodhi* tree might symbolize his enlightenment.

By the first century CE, however, when the Kushan Empire ruled most of north and northwestern India, the Mahayana school of Buddhism had brought fundamental changes to Buddhist cosmology and further connected the *sangha*, the community of Buddhist monks, with commercial communities. The Buddha was now worshipped as an omnipotent god. His transition from sage to god had begun by the reign of the Indo-Greek king Menander (also known as Milinda, late second century BCE) who, Buddhist texts report, was puzzled by the contradiction between the Buddha's human nature and his divinity (Document 9). By the time of the Kushan Empire, the divinity of the Buddha was no longer in question, and the Buddhist sangha had built monasteries surrounding the stupas, adorned with carved statues of the Buddha. Mahayana Buddhism also worshipped a host of deities called bodhisattvas, saints who had accumulated enough merit to forego another rebirth (Documents 10, 11) and were on the brink of achieving nirvana,

Figure 1. *Kushan Gold Coin, ca. 130 CE*
This coin exemplifies the diffusion of languages and amalgamation of religions that took place on the Silk Roads. The most famous Kushan king, Kanishka, is shown on one side, where in the inscription, written in a language native to northwestern India but with the Greek alphabet, reads "Great King, King of Kings, Son of God, Kanishka." On the other side is a Hindu god, four-armed Shiva. Here the Greek inscription reads "Oesho," the Bactrian name for Shiva. Coins such as these facilitated trade.

where the suffering of earthbound lives would be eliminated; the bo-dhisattvas had postponed their final emancipation to stay in this world and help all its creatures cross what they called the ocean of sufferings. These developments in the theology and institutions of Buddhism made the religion less mysterious to foreigners. Traders now worshipped the Buddha as a god and sought protections from various Buddhist deities when they came to northwestern India to trade in silk and gems.

Figure 1. (*continued*)

Thus during the rule of the Kushans, traders from the Mediterranean world and East Asia exchanged not only trade goods but also ideas. Some Roman Empire traders, often Greek-speaking Egyptians, reached Kushan territory by sea, sailing through the Red Sea and across the Arabian Sea to ports in western India. Merchants from the empire's caravan cities such as Palmyra in Syria took land routes through the Parthian Empire to Bactria and returned home with silks. The Parthian traders, descendants of the ancient Scythians, were often rivals of the Romans in the silk trade.

Kushan and Sogdian traders speaking a variety of languages traveled between China's Han Empire and India. They found hospitality, security, and interpreters at the Buddhist monasteries along the way and often made generous donations to the monasteries for the construction of additional facilities and the carving of religious sculptures. Buddhist donors also hoped that their donations would bring them religious merit, which would improve their lot in future lives as well as protect them and their loved ones in this life. Accordingly, they had their donations and their wishes inscribed on the new buildings or at the base of the sculptures (Document 12).

As traders and monks spent time together, they benefited and learned from each other. The increase in commercial activities brought prosperity not only to the Kushan state but also to the Buddhist monasteries. When the Buddha was alive, he had gone out to beg for food every day and never had a permanent residence. By Kushan times, in contrast, Buddhist monks lived in splendid settings. Instead of going out to beg for food, they set up symbolic begging bowls in front of their monasteries for the collection of valuables. Thus the monasteries came to possess silks from China; pearls from Sri Lanka and the Persian Gulf; crystal and other precious stones from India; frankincense and myrrh from Arabia; red coral, gold and silver coins, glassware, and grape wine from the Mediterranean; and lapis lazuli, a dark-blue gemstone from northeastern Afghanistan. Monks burned incense made of frankincense and myrrh to worship the Buddha and bodhisattvas; decorated stupas with silk banners and draperies, pearls, and coral and crystal beads; and painted the hair of the Buddha and bodhisattvas with pigments made from lapis lazuli.

Once these valuable goods entered Buddhist monasteries, they became sacred objects. In particular, Buddhist writers of the period accorded some of the most precious stones, which had become a significant part of the Buddhist esthetic, the status of *sapta ratana,* "the Seven Treasures," and these were said to adorn the heavens or Buddha lands. According to Mahayana theology, devotees who were not yet ready to go to nirvana after their death could hope to go to one of the many heavens of the bodhisattvas. The best known is the Western Pure Land, which is overseen by Amitabha, a bodhisattva who efficiently answers the calls of his devotees (Document 11). However, those seeking help for life on this earth worship the bodhisattva Avalokiteshvara, who assists the world's creatures, especially travelers, on land and sea (Document 10). Donating either silk or the Seven Treasures to this bodhisattva is believed to aid those in danger. Traders were willing to donate such goods from their inventories, and local devotees were happy to purchase these treasures from the monastery, since the proceeds would be used for its benefit. Mahayana Buddhist texts thus became advocates for trade in the valuable goods that traveled the Silk Roads.[6] Eventually, Mahayana Buddhism spread from India to Central Asia and China.

THE OASIS TOWNS OF CENTRAL ASIA AND THE SPREAD OF BUDDHISM, THIRD–SEVENTH CENTURIES

While the agricultural empires of China and Rome were the major markets for luxury goods, the lands of Central Asia crossed by the Silk Roads were also transformed by trade. Interactions between the steppe and the oases were, in fact, the basic dynamics of the Silk Roads. In the north on the steppe, a grassland that stretches from Mongolia to the Caspian Sea, horseback-riding nomadic tribes moved around within their own territories and could be distinguished from each other mainly by the different languages they spoke. Conflicts among the tribes and with the agricultural empires often stimulated large-scale migrations, which generally went westward, starting with the Yuezhi. In the south, the people of the Takla Makan Desert lived in oasis towns that clung to the desert's rim at the bottom of the mountains and were gradually settled by Chinese, Indian, and Central Asian immigrants as well as at least a few Greeks who had been living in Central Asia for many generations (Document 13). Although nomads sometimes raided the oases for goods and slaves, some also settled there peaceably. The people of the Takla Makan Desert were the first in Central Asia to convert to Buddhism. By the time that Buddhist monasteries appeared in these oasis towns, local agricultural production could support thousands of people.

Farther west in Ferghana, where the Syr River flows, and in Sogdiana, on the plain between the Syr and the Amu Rivers, a series of large oases had developed using river water to irrigate agricultural fields. Before the coming of the Greeks in the late fourth century BCE, the Sogdians had not been farmers, or at least not full-time farmers. Both Sogdiana and Ferghana were mainly famous for good horses. After the founding of Greek garrison towns, grape cultivation and wineries had developed along with food crops (Document 13). Thereafter the Sogdians, realizing the benefits of commerce, soon became the most active and numerous traders on the routes connecting Persia, India, and China. They must also have been intrepid mountaineers, given that the Sogdian route to India went over the extremely dangerous high-altitude passes of the upper Indus Valley. Their first encounter with Buddhism was in the region of Gandhara, and they carried its teachings back to Sogdiana. Some early Sogdian Buddhists

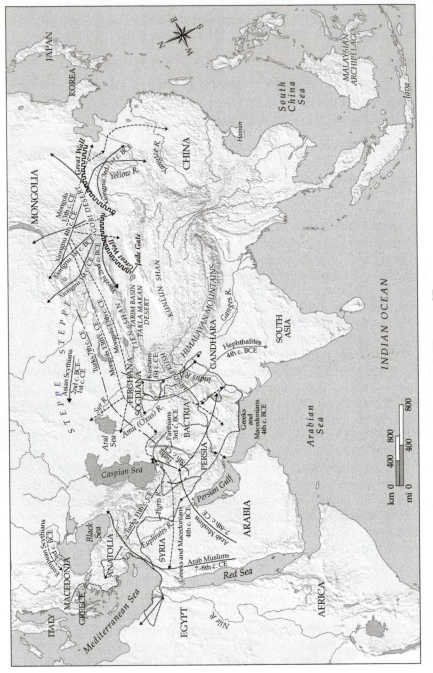

Map 2. *Migrations and Conquests on the Silk Roads, 350 BCE–1300 CE*

also went to China to trade and in Luoyang helped to translate Buddhist texts into Chinese. In fact, several of the earliest Buddhist preachers in China had the surname Kang, the name the Chinese authorities gave to people from Kangju, their name for Sogdiana.

Nevertheless, Buddhist institutions did not take root in China or Central Asia until the late third century, after the Han Empire had collapsed, the Roman Empire had started to decline, and Rome's market for eastern luxuries had withered. It was around this time that Buddhist monasteries began to appear in many oases between Sogdiana and Turfan, only three hundred miles west of China's Jade Gate. Although few monks engaged in agricultural work, they were active members of the community and very much involved in transactions between the local people and outsiders (Document 13). They often served as interpreters, since the populations in the Central Asian oases had diverse origins and no single language was used for all occasions.

Meanwhile, even though the Han dynasty had fallen, relatively small regional states in northern China continued to exert an influence in the towns of the Takla Makan Desert. For example, in Khotan, an oasis on its southern edge, local rulers issued bilingual coins. On one side the inscription was written in the Prakrit language, a vernacular related to Sanskrit in India, with the Kharoshthi script, and on the other side the inscription was in Chinese written with Chinese characters. Sogdian traders continued to travel to China and settled in a great many oases along the Silk Roads, and whenever the demand for luxuries in China was weak due to civil wars, they engaged in regional trade from oasis to oasis (Document 14).

During the fourth century, nomads set off a large wave of migration and invasion to their south. Among them were the Xiongnu, who managed to pass through the Great Wall and migrate into northern China, where during its civil wars they built a series of ephemeral states. Eventually, the Tuoba family of the Xianbei people, who were originally from Mongolia, established the Northern Wei dynasty (386–534). They thus became rulers of a part of agricultural China, and they changed their surname to the Chinese name Yuan. Meanwhile, another nomadic group, the Hephthalites, or White Huns, occupied a number of Central Asian oases and made incursions into India. They also, in due course, transformed themselves into rulers and residents of sedentary societies. These rulers of nomadic background soon learned the benefits of patronizing religious institutions, especially Buddhist monasteries, for communicating with their subjects and for enhancing their legitimacy. It was at this time that Buddhist cave monasteries with their numerous murals and sculptures lined the foothills of the Central Asian trade routes. The two gigantic standing-Buddha statues at Bamiyan, in the Hindu Kush Valley, became a landmark at the western end of the Central Asian Silk Road, until they were destroyed by the Taliban in 2001. And at Yungang, in northeastern China in the foothills near the Great Wall, five huge sitting Buddhas marked the eastern end of the Central Asian Silk Road.[7] Between them were a series of fourth-century Buddhist cave temples, including Kezil, near modern Kucha on the northern edge of the Takla Makan Desert, and Dunhuang, just inside the Jade Gate.

During this time, Chinese Buddhist monks began traveling to India to learn the true Buddhist doctrines firsthand. Faxian, for example, made a pilgrimage to India from 399 to 414 (Document 15), and Xuanzang made one from 629 to 645 (Document 17). These religious travelers were significant carriers of goods along the Silk Roads. Xuanzang's pilgrimage is a good example. When he left Turfan, he needed an entire caravan of horses to carry his provisions and travel funds, which were mostly bolts of silk damask. After he returned to China, he sent many of the gifts he received from the emperor—mostly silk textiles and robes—to his Indian friends through various traders. He also returned with Buddhist sutras and Sanskrit texts, which he translated. In the early sixth century, the Northern Wei sent a mission to deliver tribute to Buddhist shrines in Central Asia and India (Document 16). These pilgrims witnessed the further development of Buddhism in Central Asia and took advantage of the hospitality offered by the region's monasteries. At a time when the newly established Tang Empire (618–907) had not yet extended its power into Central Asia, the oases and steppe powers provided a thoroughfare for travelers, both traders and monks. After the Tang expanded, it acted as the great patron of the Silk Roads.

For more than four centuries, between the Han Empire's withdrawal from Central Asia and the Tang Empire's extension in its eastern parts, Buddhist monasteries dominated this region and shaped the religious mentality as well as the economic behavior of its people. Here, and later in Tang China, the acceptance of Buddhism changed burial practices. From ancient times, the Chinese had buried the deceased's precious possessions with the body, believing that an individual would live another life after death and that all a person owned in this world could be carried over into the next life. But Buddhism taught that one would be reborn as another sort of creature after death, so people ceased burying goods with the body. Instead, the virtues and merits of the dead were recorded and buried with the deceased (Document 18), and good deeds, especially donations to Buddhist monasteries, were believed to secure a better rebirth.

THE BYZANTINE EMPIRE AND SILKS IN ROYAL PURPLE, SIXTH–NINTH CENTURIES

After the disintegration of the western part of the Roman Empire in the fifth century, the eastern part survived as the Byzantine Empire, and its capital of Constantinople emerged as the Mediterranean region's major sponsor of the trade in eastern luxuries. This city, once called Byzantium, had been renamed by Emperor Constantine (r. 306–337), who made it an imperial capital. Constantine had also made Christianity a legal religion, as he clearly saw a compatibility between a monotheistic religion and the authoritarian power of a Roman emperor. In the following centuries, emperors in Constantinople became the staunch supporters and patrons of the Christian church and were deeply involved in the religion's theological development.

In the years between the high point of the Roman Empire and the peak of Byzantine power, the technology and marketing of silk textiles had changed fundamentally. In Pliny's time, women preferred the light crepe imported from China, and men wore wool dyed in prestigious purple. Persians, both the Parthian rivals of the Romans and the Sassanids who defeated the Parthians and ruled Persia until the Arab conquest of the seventh century, liked heavy silk tapestries. The Persians had a long tradition of rug weaving, and once silk yarn became available they adapted their looms to create silk tapestries that were often superior to Chinese products. The process required sophisticated technology and highly skilled artisans, but not the finest of silk fibers. Soon weavers in Gaza, Beirut, and other Roman cities on the eastern shore of the Mediterranean started to weave their textiles the Persian way. When they could not get enough silk yarn from China, they bought plain silk tabby and unraveled it to get the fibers they needed for their looms.

The Byzantine Empire had a world monopoly on the rare purple dye made from eastern Mediterranean shellfish, and the custom developed that the emperor should wear purple. Not only should his ritual robes be purple, but he should be born in purple—that is, in a chamber built with purple stones—and be buried in a sarcophagus of purple stone. Because the shellfish's purple dye works well on silk fibers, as both are animal proteins, purple-colored silks became the most expensive and prestigious clothing for both women and men in the Byzantine Empire and the Christian world. In the sixth century, the Byzantine emperor Justinian (r. 527–565) and his advisers decided that both resources could serve political purposes, and thus they decreed that within the empire the shellfish-dyed purple silks could be worn only by the emperor and his court.

Justinian was notable for recovering some Roman territories in the West that had been lost to various invaders and also for promoting the development of sericulture—the technology of raising silkworms, harvesting the filaments from the cocoons, and spinning silk thread. Although the transfer of this technology to the West is popularly attributed to Nestorian Christian monks asked by the emperor to smuggle silkworm eggs out of China (Document 19), this story is unlikely, as discussed in the headnote to Document 19. The work started by Justinian no doubt took many decades to accomplish,[8] but what is certain is that Byzantine rulers did everything they could to monopolize the production and distribution of silk textiles within their realm (Documents 20, 21). Silk consumption and production became one of the empire's many tools for the display and consolidation of imperial power.

Justinian's ambition was to be not only the emperor of the area that had been the entire Roman Empire but also the leader of the Christian world. During his reign, purple silk textiles also became an efficient diplomatic tool to exert his influence within the Christian church. One of his most obvious achievements in support of Christianity was the construction of a monumental cathedral, the Hagia Sophia, whose mosaics display purple as a sacred color. Subsequently, the Byzantines added a provision in the sumptuary law—the law regulating dress, food, and certain privileges to particular classes—granting Christian priests and churches the right to wear and use silk textiles and robes. Byzantine silk culture set the standard of adornment and display for all Christian churches and thereby contributed to believers' vision of heaven.

Shortly after sericulture was established in the eastern Mediterranean, the part of Anatolia where mulberry trees flourished was conquered by Arabs, who were extending their control of the region in the name of the new religion of Islam. Although this was a significant loss for the Byzantines, the traders who lived in Anatolia and Syria, then

---

Opposite: **Figure 2.** *Hagia Sophia Mosaic, Constantinople, late tenth century CE*
This gold and glass mosaic is situated above the royal entrance to the Hagia Sophia in Constantinople (today Istanbul). It shows the Virgin Mary, the patron saint of Constantinople, robed in purple with the baby Jesus on her lap. On her right Justinian holds a model of the cathedral, and on her left Constantine holds a model of the city of Constantinople. Both emperors are robed at least in part in purple, thus displaying the role of purple silk in marking a celestial and an earthly hierarchy. Mary, robed fully in purple, is presented as the highest authority, and the two emperors are portrayed as those closest to her in significance and the most important benefactors of the Christian church.

also under Muslim rule, continued to sell silk materials and textiles to customers in Constantinople and other Byzantine cities (Document 21).

Due to the efforts of the Muslim powers, sericulture now spread throughout the entire Mediterranean region, and the Byzantine government could no longer control the production and consumption of silk textiles. The focus of the Byzantine monopoly then became the production and supply of the purple shellfish dye, which were easier to control. The government watched every step of its production and transport, and thereby managed to keep the process secret for many more centuries. During the reign of Emperor Leo VI (r. 886–912), the mayor of Constantinople guarded the monopoly forcefully (Document 21). Even after the empire had shrunk to a small and weak state following the devastation wrought by the Christian Crusaders in the thirteenth century, the Byzantine rulers managed to maintain their monopoly of the purple dye. Thus the prestige of wearing purple-hued silk robes did not end until the total collapse of the Byzantine Empire in the fifteenth century.

THE TANG EMPIRE AND FOREIGN TRADERS AND PRIESTS, EIGHTH–TENTH CENTURIES

The Tang Empire (618–907 CE) brought another celebrated imperial age to China, and its prestige made it a cultural model for nearby countries such as Korea and Japan as well as for several Central Asian states. The Tang capital at Chang'an and secondary capital at Luoyang attracted many foreign students of Confucianism, Buddhism, and other subjects. The large market for imported luxury goods drew foreign traders to sell their goods and Chinese traders to engage in foreign trade (Document 22). Foreign travelers established their own neighborhoods in the cities of China, and some enjoyed the patronage of the imperial court. Court documents record foreign envoys carrying tribute gifts to Chang'an, and figurines portray these people's non-Chinese faces and clothing styles.

Following Xuanzang's famous seventh-century pilgrimage, many Chinese Buddhist monks also went to India to look for Buddhist texts and relics of the Buddha. Nevertheless, even during the Tang dynasty, Buddhism never gained the status of a state religion as Christianity had in the Byzantine Empire. Yet since all travelers, regardless of religion, took advantage of the hospitality found in Buddhist monasteries and other religious hostels, their donations facilitated more excavations of caves adorned with more religious paintings and sculptures.

Figure 3. *Glazed Figurine of Camel and Rider, Tang dynasty, eighth century CE*
This *sancai* (tricolor) glazed figurine is typical of burial goods popular during
the Tang dynasty. Here the exaggerated large nose indicates that the camel
rider is not Chinese, but Central Asian. Other figurines portray African and
Greek riders, but the vast majority of the Silk Roads trade was handled by the
peoples of Central Asia, primarily Sogdians.

Like the Byzantine Empire, its contemporary, the Tang Empire also
tried to monopolize the production and use of the most prestigious silk
textiles for political purposes. Since the Han dynasty, commoners had
been banned from wearing silk tapestries and embroidered silk clothes,
and in the seventh century the newly established Tang Empire reas-
serted similar sumptuary laws for a new reason. Tang rulers sought

to overcome local hereditary powers and end inefficiency by building a new, merit-based bureaucracy in which only highly educated men would serve as officials. To enhance the prestige of the new scholar-bureaucrats, the emperors prescribed acceptable clothing for various categories of people, designating particular patterns and a particular color for the official robes worn by each level of the bureaucratic hierarchy. Only the ritual robes of the emperors remained yellow, traditionally the royal color in China since ancient times. Among their advisers and officials, the color that was assigned the highest status was purple, the same color that the Byzantines were using to distinguish their imperial family. The purple dye used in Tang China was an indigenous product, but the aesthetic value of purple could have been influenced by the Roman Empire and Byzantium, as purple had not previously been a favored color in China. Once the color purple was established as the most prestigious within the bureaucratic ranks, all those who aspired to move up in society dreamed of wearing it (Document 22).

Like the Byzantine rulers, the Tang emperors also displayed their patronage of religious personages and institutions by granting purple robes. However, the Tang emperors never tried to establish a single state religion. Instead, they rewarded individual priests and institutions, regardless of religion, for their service to the court and the state. Clearly Buddhism enjoyed the most patronage from the royal families and the most support from commoners, but Buddhism had a strong competitor in Daoism. The Tang ruling family claimed a close relationship to Daoism, but enlisted the services of priests from many different religions—Buddhists and even Hindu Brahmans as well as Daoists—in praying for the empress during childbirth, for example, and for military victories on the frontier. Those called upon accumulated large quantities of purple robes as well as other fine robes and silk textiles. Members of religious institutions, especially Buddhists, often breached the government's sumptuary rules by selling the restricted goods granted to them by the royal family for cash in local markets. It was largely for this reason that the Tang silk monopoly declined and disappeared when the dynasty ended.

During the golden age of the Tang, however, Nestorian Christians, Zoroastrians, Manichaeans, and Muslims all gained followers in China. Nestorianism, a Christian sect based in Syria and condemned for heresy by a Byzantine church council in 431, found an auspicious setting for the propagation of Christianity in the Tang Empire. In 635, A-luo-ben (Rabban), the first recorded Nestorian missionary to settle in China, reached Chang'an, and in 638 he established a church there with the

Tang government's permission (Document 23). The Nestorian church flourished in Tang China for more than two hundred years and received many grants of silks from Tang emperors. One priest was even honored with a purple robe. Records of the Tang courts also indicate that Constantinople sent a number of Orthodox Christian archbishops to China, but they do not seem to have had much impact.

Zoroastrian priests were also active in Chinese cities. Zoroastrianism was an ancient Persian religion that had lost much of its significance during the rule of the Parthians. However, after the Sassanids recovered Persia in the third century CE, it became the official religion. Its presence in Tang China was, however, largely owing to Sogdians, who seem to have been open to numerous religions, especially those practiced by foreign traders. The Sogdians had been among the first Buddhists to arrive in China; from as early as the fifth century, even before China was reunified and the Tang dynasty was founded, most Sogdians who went to China to trade were Zoroastrians. Although the Sogdian Zoroastrians joined the Tang army and served as Tang officials, their religion does not seem to have attracted many Chinese converts. Their religious activities tended toward the mystical and magical, and even though Zoroastrian priests performed various rituals in public that attracted much curiosity, Chinese crowds had little or no understanding of their religious meanings (Document 22).[9]

The Sogdians were also indirectly responsible for the arrival of the Manichaean religion in China. Manichaeism first emerged in Persia in the second century CE. Mani, its founder, had been influenced by both Buddhism and Christianity, and this religion eventually had a significant presence from the shores of the Mediterranean to China. The people who brought it to China were the Uighurs, a nomadic Turkish tribe whose pastures were located along China's northern frontier. Like their nomadic predecessors, they traded their horses for Chinese silks, but they had difficulty finding a market for the amount of silk that they were receiving. Thus they began to use Sogdian traders as their agents. These Sogdians were Manichaeans, and they converted their Uighur business partners to this religion. Thereafter, the Manichaean temples that appeared in Tang cities served as trading depots for both the Uighurs and their Sogdian agents. As the rituals of Manichaeism were somewhat similar to those of Buddhism, its priests may have been more successful than the Zoroastrians in attracting Chinese converts.

On the Silk Roads, trade and religion seemed inseparable, and pilgrims and priests carried goods and generated trade. The Sogdians were not only successful and pragmatic traders but also faithful propagators of their religions. In Sogdiana they decorated their homes with inspirational murals from many different religions as well as from secular traditions. In their trading diasporas, they often followed the religious trends of the time, and they used both Zoroastrian temples and Manichaean shrines to practice their faith and to carry out their business.

When, late in the Tang dynasty, the empire's economy declined, Emperor Wuzong (r. 841–847) blamed its troubles on foreign religious institutions that had appropriated much wealth and land, and eventually he banished all foreign religious institutions from China, including those of the Buddhists (Document 24). This drastic policy began over a conflict with the Uighurs and what Wuzong claimed was an imbalance in the horse-silk trade that was causing the economic decline. He banned their Manichaean religion and in 845 extended his attacks to all foreign religions. He closed Buddhist monasteries, confiscated their properties, and sent monks back to their homes, whether they were from outside or inside the empire. Within in a very short time, however, he had to restore the Buddhist institutions, for it soon became obvious that neither the state nor the Chinese people could function without the many services that the Buddhist monasteries provided. Wuzong ruled for only a few years. Buddhism recovered fully after his reign, but the other religions either disappeared from China or retreated to remote areas.

MUSLIM BAGHDAD IN THE EURASIAN MARKET, NINTH–ELEVENTH CENTURIES

After the emergence of Islam on the Arabian Peninsula in the early seventh century, friction between its leaders and nearby empires soon led to hostilities and, thereafter, to the Muslim conquest of large portions of Eurasia and Africa. These conquests obviously had a major political impact, but also important were the economic changes they brought. Islam introduced a new set of aesthetic values regarding material culture. In its early days, Islam frowned upon luxuries, and so its spread had a significant impact on the marketing of silks and other Silk Roads goods. Because this religion maintains that all people are equal before God, Muslim society rejected both the religious and the political hierarchies that then flourished, as well as the restrictions and material symbols that marked their ranks. Muslims and their converts thus discontinued many of the Byzantine and Tang practices regarding the wearing of silk.

The ruling caliphs of Islam, known as the commanders of the faithful, also changed practices regarding the production of silk in territories they seized from the Byzantines and the Persian Sassanids. Silk-weaving was no longer a royal monopoly, and the caliphs did not control the production of even the rarest and most valuable silk textiles, such as those dyed purple and brocades made with golden threads. Aesthetically, Muslims strongly disliked the color purple, which they called the "blood color." The caliphate did order all weaving shops to inscribe silk products with a sentence praising Allah, as well as the place and time of production and the name of the vizier, or prime minister, who was in charge of taxation. This practice, called the *tiraz*, put a specific "brand name" on every textile product, facilitating the government's ability to tax the industry and the market and to supervise the quality of the product. The unintended result of this policy was the development of a brand-oriented market that created a new dynamic in textile production and distribution.

The Prophet Muhammad and early Muslims were Arabs, either the residents of towns known for their caravan traders or Bedouin nomads who lived in tents as they moved their herds from one locale to another. Even after they became rulers of agricultural societies, they preferred their tent culture, and so they decorated their urban palaces and mansions with the same sort of upholsteries and rugs they had used to furnish their tents. In short, they moved their tent culture into their palaces. Outside the Arabian Peninsula, the first Muslim political center — the capital of the Umayyad Caliphate — had been at Damascus in Syria, where Arabic languages were indigenous. After a civil war within the ranks of the caliphate in the middle of the eighth century, the political center of the Muslim empire moved eastward to Baghdad — the capital of the Abbasid Caliphate — which had been ruled for centuries by the Persian Sassanids. Thereafter, Muslims who spoke Persian asserted their economic as well as their political influence.

Persians had a long tradition of weaving woolen and silk carpets and tapestries, and their textiles soon came to dominate the market in home furnishings (Document 27). Carpets and tapestries brightened the brick and pebble walls of the palaces and mansions of the caliphs and princes in Baghdad, Samara, and other cities,[10] and bureaucrats, generals, and wealthy residents were soon caught up in this fashion trend, especially as there was no sumptuary law that forbade their using the same luxurious materials that the caliphs used. Thus, in the Muslim world, the market for textiles, especially silk textiles, expanded rapidly.

The Abbasid Caliphate soon incorporated yet another nomadic material culture that put a high value on textiles. Turkic tribes, originally from the Mongolian steppe, were now migrating westward, and they, too, became involved in the political and economic dynamics of the Muslim world. As early as the seventh century, this Turkish migration had already reached Sogdiana in Central Asia. After the Abbasid conquest of Central Asia in the eighth century, many Turks moved to Baghdad to pursue civic, intellectual, and military careers within the Abbasid Caliphate. The Turkish soldiers' bravery and sturdiness were well known. Thus, when the caliph Mu'tasim (r. 833–842) believed he was being oppressed by court politicians, he brought Turkish slave-soldiers, recruited from captured slaves or war prisoners, into Baghdad to serve his needs (Document 26). The Turkish tribes, still moving westward, thus had even more access to the center of power in the Muslim world and eventually became the major force battling the Christian Crusades.

Islamic institutions had only a marginal role in the large markets of northern China, but Muslim merchants actively traded in the ports of China's southern coast, where they arrived by sea. In Canton they established their own neighborhood, where they traded and practiced their religion (Document 25). During the Tang religious persecution of the mid-ninth century, the Muslim community in China suffered relatively little due to its limited presence in the capital region, and the Muslim merchant community in Canton was largely immune. But it was almost wiped out during an uprising of southern peasants that eventually brought down the Tang dynasty. Some of the Muslim merchants who survived the rebellion moved their establishments to Quanzhou, a port north of Canton, near modern Xiamen in the province of Fujian.

TRADE NETWORKS FROM THE MEDITERRANEAN TO THE SOUTH CHINA SEA, TENTH–THIRTEENTH CENTURIES

By the tenth century, Muslim traders had created large mercantile networks that connected the Mediterranean to the east coast of Africa and to various ports in the Indian Ocean, in Southeast Asia, and on the South China Sea. From that time on, sea routes south of Eurasia gradually replaced land routes as the main commercial artery of trade. This fundamental change in trading patterns was not a result of warfare or political instability, nor was it due to the weakness of economies. Throughout the centuries that the Silk Roads had flourished, continuous warfare and political upheavals never stopped trade. However, agricultural developments from East Asia to western Europe had created wealthy societies and thus more surpluses for trade. Now staple goods such as cotton textiles, rice and other grains, timber, tea, and porcelain and ceramics became part of long-distance trade in addition to highly valued luxuries such as silks, gemstones, and fragrances. These staple goods were bulky, such as tea, or heavy, such as timber, or fragile, such as porcelain, which had to be packed in heavy crates. Overland caravans could not manage their transport. Meanwhile, ships had been improved for long-distance seafaring, and merchant communities in many countries thus increasingly depended on ships to carry their goods.

Three ports served as the key depots for this extensive maritime trading network. In the west, Cairo linked the Mediterranean traffic to ships on the Red and Arabian Seas. After Baghdad lost control of some of its distant territories, the Fatimids, a Shiite Muslim lineage, arose in North Africa and took over Egypt in 969. In very little time, Cairo became a new center of Muslim culture. Muslim and Jewish trading communities that migrated to Cairo oversaw the transport of goods arriving at Alexandria by ship, mostly from Italy, and then up the Nile River to Cairo. From there, these goods were dispatched overland to ports on the Red Sea, where they were loaded onto ships bound for India.

The ships that plied the Arabian Sea were called dhows. They were medium-sized vessels with triangular sails, later known as a lateen rig. Since ancient times, Arab peoples on the southern coasts of the peninsula had sailed the Arabian Sea, taking advantage of the monsoon winds. Once the dhows anchored at Quilon (in modern-day Kerala), the designated port on India's southwest coast, the traders unloaded their cargo. Hindu chiefs in Quilon welcomed foreign traders, especially Muslim traders. During the tenth and eleventh centuries, this coast was under the dominion of the Chola Empire based in southeastern India. Quilon was, nevertheless, a haven of commerce where traders from the West could sell their goods to the local people or to traders who came on ships from as far away as China. Quilon's markets were filled with valuable and often rare goods from many lands.

The ships that came to Quilon from China were known as "junks." They were huge vessels built with transverse bulkheads that made them especially strong. Horizontal partitions in the holds created sealed compartments that would keep a ship afloat even if one compartment was damaged and filled with water. In Quilon, traders could board junks bound for Quanzhou on China's southeastern coast. The Song dynasty (960–1279) moved its import-export office from Canton to Quanzhou to collect taxes and to guide and protect ships entering and leaving the port (Document 29). The Yuan dynasty (1279–1368), which was established by the Mongols, a power that first arose from the steppe under Genghis Khan (1167?–1227), followed the same policies. Genghis Khan's grandson, Khubilai Khan (1215–1294), declared himself the first Yuan emperor and encouraged foreign commerce (Document 34). In the process of conquering China, the Mongols had to build a navy and learn the craft of shipbuilding. They also tried to become a sea power. Although their efforts to conquer Japan and Java failed, they were efficient at collecting revenue from the maritime trade centered in the port of Quanzhou.

Commercial communities from many countries were active in all three ports, where traders of various religious affiliations found hospitality and set up their own facilities. Quanzhou, especially, was a haven for traders from a wide variety of religious communities. The Mongols had their own financial systems and stationed representatives and agents in all the ports, and they frequently formed close commercial relationships with trading firms of other nationalities. These trading communities, not the governments, controlled the commercial activity.

Muslim traders owned most of the ships on the Mediterranean Sea, which were based in North African ports, and the dhows on the Arabian Sea.[11] To safeguard navigation on the Arabian Sea, the Fatimid government in Cairo started an armed escort system called the *karim*. Three or four armed vessels regularly guarded merchant fleets going to and from India. Since their departures were regularly scheduled, merchants who did not own ships could sail on the karim ships or put their cargos on them for delivery elsewhere. Traders who joined the karim trade were known as *karimi*s. Usually they were family trading firms who assigned their goods and staffs to the fleets. In the Muslim community, the only obstacle to trade was the Islamic prohibition on moneylending, especially on collecting interest on loans. To avoid the stigma of moneylending, Muslims created partnerships between financiers and the traders who traveled with their goods. When a trader returned from a commercial voyage with a profit, he paid back the money he had borrowed and also shared the profit with his partner. If the goods were lost due to shipwrecks or other unpredictable events, the loss was shared. This credit system worked well and was copied by others, including Jewish traders.

At this time, a Jewish community based in Fustat, the old part of Cairo, was also very much involved in the maritime trade on the Mediterranean and Arabian Seas. Jewish traders owned large consignments that they put on ships owned by Muslims, and they also boarded karim ships destined for ports on the Arabian Sea. Jewish traders had a relatively good relationship with the Fatimids, and some even collected the government's taxes from the local people in the areas around the North African ports where they traded. Jewish bankers also played an essential role in the long-distance trade, since they were experts in sorting and evaluating coins from many different lands. Jewish traders who lived in Arabic lands learned to speak and write in Arabic, but when corresponding with each other they wrote Arabic in the Hebrew script (Document 31). Jews generally lived peacefully under the Muslim caliphates. Although a few Muslim rulers occasionally restricted their business or religious activities, Jews could still pursue profits and purchase and enjoy whatever luxuries they desired, including silk clothing (Document 28).

Cairo traders, including Jews, Coptic Christians, and Muslims, shared similar commercial ethics and practices and generally cooperated with each other. Their religious calendars were different, however. When traveling on the land routes, each group ceased work on a different holy day — Muslims on Friday, Jews on Saturday, and Christians on Sunday. Because of these differences, determining ships' departure schedules was a complicated matter until the Coptic Christian calendar was adopted by all the trading communities.

During the time of the Fatimids, merchants from Venice, and then from other Italian cities, came to Alexandria to buy silk, paper, and spices. There they learned trading techniques and banking practices from Jewish and Muslim traders. The Venetians also built ships, which they supplied to the Crusaders of western Europe, who, beginning in 1096, sought to reconquer Jerusalem and sacred shrines in the Holy Land that were now in the hands of Muslim Turks. Their campaigns, which continued into the thirteenth century, were ultimately a failure, although at various times they captured Jerusalem and ruled Crusader states in Palestine. Despite the warfare, the Crusaders did not hinder trade (Document 30). In fact, once they learned the real sources of spices and textiles, they actually stimulated trade. Demand for these goods and for a new "spice" called sugar increased in western Europe upon their return, and Italian merchants grew rich and powerful from this trade. In 1271, Marco Polo, a trader from Venice, set off with his father and uncle on a journey to the Mongol court of Khubilai Khan, and his report of their travels on his return more than twenty years later did much to stimulate interest in China and its riches for generations to come (Document 33).

In Quanzhou, Muslims formed a large community that dominated trade. The largest shipping firms in Quanzhou were owned by several different Muslim families, who had purchased thousands of junks from their Chinese manufacturers to maintain connections with Muslim communities in Arabia, Persia, and the islands of Southeast Asia. The eminent Muslim families residing in Quanzhou served the interests of the court during Song times, but immediately switched their loyalty to the Mongol Yuan dynasty when the latter took over the country. They acted as the new regime's liaison to overseas trading partners, using their Islamic networks and language skills (Document 34). Jewish merchants also migrated to Quanzhou and to other parts of China. Nestorian Christians, who had been expelled from China during the late Tang, reestablished themselves under Mongol rule in the thirteenth century, and they, too, became active in the maritime trade. Manichaeans, also suppressed by the late Tang persecution, had survived in southeastern China, and they likewise became active traders. There were also Hindu traders from India on China's southeastern coast. They must have found it hard to explain to the Chinese that they were not Buddhists, but members of a separate (not to mention competing) religion, and they apparently failed to get this message across. Enshrined in the largest Buddhist monastery in Quanzhou are statues of the Hindu deities Vishnu, Shiva, and Hanuman, an example of the religious diffusion often evident in trading communities.

Literally tons of herbs, spices, and aromatic resins used to make incense as well as medicines arrived at Quanzhou by ship. These items were no longer only for the use of religious institutions and royal families, but were commodities sold in even the most ordinary markets of China (Document 32). Large numbers of people in Asia and in the Mediterranean world were now wealthy enough to use spices in their cooking, incense in their devotions, and medicines made with imported herbs. Shiploads of silk textiles, tea, and porcelain departed from the port of Quanzhou. Some were highly valued products for the elites, and some were affordable for ordinary people to use, at least on some occasions.

Thus after fifteen hundred years of the Silk Roads, even as traffic shifted from the old land routes to the sea, the trade that had begun as an imperial exchange for rare luxuries was now driven by commerce and profit and by the desires of ordinary people rather than only by elites. As the trade broadened and widened, so did exchange of ideas, religions, and technologies. With the West ever more interested in the commodities of the East, and merchants and sailors ever more adventuresome in their search for new routes and higher profits, the stage was set for the modern era.

NOTES

[1] For the variety of silk textiles from Han China, see Adreas Schmidt-Clinet, Annemarie Stauffer, and Khaled Al-As'ad, *Die Textilien aus Palmyra* (Mainz am Rhein: Verlag Philipp von Zabern, 2000), especially for the numerous high-quality plates and figures that reveal the styles of the second century CE.

[2] This Yumen, sometimes seen on maps as Yumenguan, was located west of Dunhuang and should not be confused with the present-day city of Yumen, which is located east of Dunhuang.

[3] For information regarding this international trade studied from the perspective of the Roman Empire, see Gary K. Young, *Rome's Eastern Trade: International Commerce and Imperial Policy, 31 BC–AD 305* (London and New York: Routledge, 2001).

[4] This number is probably an estimation by Zhang Qian and was recorded by Sima Qian. Sima Qian, *Records of the Grand Historian of China*, trans. Burton Watson (New York: Columbia University Press, 1961), 2: 267.

[5] The excavations of Tillya Tepe in Afghanistan revealed a wealth of golden ornaments and other valuable goods that were buried with the Kushan rulers. See Victor Sardini, *The Golden Hoard of Bactria* (New York: Harry N. Abrams, and Leningrad: Aurora Art Publishers, 1985).

[6] For an analysis of the relationship between the theological development of Mahayana Buddhism and the Silk Road trade, see Xinru Liu, *Ancient India and Ancient China: Trade and Religious Exchanges, AD 1–600* (New Delhi: Oxford University Press, 1988), 88–102.

[7] For a good survey of Buddhist cave monasteries and their engagement in trade, see Annette L. Juliano and Judith A. Lerner, eds., *Monks and Merchants: Silk Road Treasures from Northwest China* (New York: Harry N. Abrams, with the Asia Society, 2001).

[8] For a comprehensive analysis of the Byzantine silk industry and its political significance, see R. S. Lopez, "Silk Industry in the Byzantine Empire," *Speculum* 20 (1945): 1–43.

[9] Étienne de la Vaissière, *Sogdian Traders: A History*, trans. James Ward (Leiden: Brill Academic Publishers, 2005), is a collection of essays on recent discoveries of Sogdian graves and remains in China.

[10] Hugh Kennedy describes the splendid court decoration when the caliph Muqtadir received a delegation from Constantinople in 917. See *When Baghdad Ruled the Muslim World* (Cambridge, Mass.: Da Capo Press, 2005), 152–56.

[11] For more technical details about Arab dhows and seafaring, see George Fadlo Hourani, *Arab Seafaring in the Indian Ocean in Ancient and Early Medieval Times*, rev. and expanded by John Carswell (Princeton, N.J.: Princeton University Press, 1995).

The Documents

The Decision

1

China's Trade on the Western Frontier, Second–First Centuries BCE

1

SIMA QIAN

Records of the Grand Historian of China

Early First Century BCE

Sima Qian (ca. 145–ca. 86 BCE) was court historian during the reign of Wudi (r. 140–87 BCE) of the Han dynasty. He was also an astrologer and adviser, and he intended his compilation of historical data to provide sound history lessons to the emperors. To present events as close to the truth as possible, he relied on the imperial archives under his custody, including files inherited from previous regimes and reports from officials stationed all over the empire. The narrative tradition he developed, which included the use of dialogue based on the records, influenced later Chinese historians, and Sima Qian is recognized as the father of Chinese historiography. During his time, the nomadic tribes on the steppe north of agricultural China had long been engaged with the Chinese as both adversaries and trading partners. In his Records of the Grand Historian of China, *Sima Qian used reports from frontier officers to detail the politics of the Xiongnu tribal confederation, the dominant power on the steppe, and the conflicts and commercial exchanges between the Xiongnu and the Chinese dynasties that ruled from the fourth to the second centuries BCE. This excerpt describes interactions between the Xiongnu and other nomadic peoples, and with the Han dynasty. How would this account differ if it had been written by the nomads?*

Sima Qian, *Records of the Grand Historian of China*, trans. Burton Watson (New York: Columbia University Press, 1961), 2:160–66.

Finally Ch'in[1] overthrew the other six states, and the First Emperor of the Ch'in dispatched Meng T'ien to lead a force of a hundred thousand men north to attack the barbarians. He seized control of all the lands south of the Yellow River and established border defenses along the river, constructing forty-four walled district cities overlooking the river and manning them with convict laborers transported to the border for garrison duty. He also built the Direct Road from Chiu-yüan to Yün-yang. Thus he utilized the natural mountain barriers to establish the border defenses, scooping out the valleys and constructing ramparts and building installations at other points where they were needed. The whole line of defenses stretched over ten thousand *li* from Lin-t'ao to Liao-tung and even extended across the Yellow River and through Yang-shan and Pei-chia.

At this time the Eastern Barbarians[2] were very powerful and the Yüeh-chih[3] were likewise flourishing. The *Shan-yü* or chieftain of the Hsiung-nu[4] was named T'ou-man. T'ou-man, unable to hold out against the Ch'in forces, had withdrawn to the far north, where he lived with his subjects for over ten years. After Meng T'ien died and the feudal lords revolted against the Ch'in, plunging China into a period of strife and turmoil, the convicts which the Ch'in had sent to the northern border to garrison the area all returned to their homes. The Hsiung-nu, the pressure against them relaxed, once again began to infiltrate south of the bend of the Yellow River until they had established themselves along the old border of China.

T'ou-man's oldest son, the heir apparent to his position, was named Mo-tun, but the *Shan-yü* also had a younger son by another consort whom he had taken later and was very fond of. He decided that he wanted to get rid of Mo-tun and set up his younger son as heir instead, and he therefore sent Mo-tun as a hostage to the Yüeh-chih nation. Then, after Mo-tun had arrived among the Yüeh-chih, T'ou-man made a sudden attack on them. The Yüeh-chih were about to kill Mo-tun in retaliation, but he managed to steal one of their best horses and escape, eventually making his way back home. His father, struck by his bravery, put him in command of a force of ten thousand cavalry.

Mo-tun had some arrows made that whistled in flight and used them to drill his troops in shooting from horseback. "Shoot wherever you see

---

[1] Qin. Because this translation of Sima Qian uses Wade-Giles romanization, significant proper names are converted to pinyin in footnotes.
[2] Nomadic group in Mongolia, east of the territory of the Xiongnu.
[3] Yuezhi.
[4] Xiongnu.

my whistling arrow strike!" he ordered, "and anyone who fails to shoot
will be cut down!" Then he went out hunting for birds and animals, and
if any of his men failed to shoot at what he himself had shot at, he cut
them down on the spot. After this, he shot a whistling arrow at one of
his best horses. Some of his men hung back and did not dare shoot
at the horse, whereupon Mo-tun at once executed them. A little later
he took an arrow and shot at his favorite wife. Again some of his men
shrank back in terror and failed to discharge their arrows, and again he
executed them on the spot. Finally he went out hunting with his men
and shot a whistling arrow at one of his father's finest horses. All his followers promptly discharged their arrows in the same direction, and Mo-
tun knew that at last they could be trusted. Accompanying his father, the
Shan-yü T'ou-man, on a hunting expedition, he shot a whistling arrow at
his father and every one of his followers aimed their arrows in the same
direction and shot the *Shan-yü* dead. Then Mo-tun executed his step-
mother, his younger brother, and all the high officials of the nation who
refused to take orders from him, and set himself up as the new *Shan-yü*.

At this time the Eastern Barbarians were very powerful and, hearing
that Mo-tun had killed his father and made himself leader, they sent an
envoy to ask if they could have T'ou-man's famous horse that could run
a thousand *li* in one day. Mo-tun consulted his ministers, but they all
replied, "The thousand-*li* horse is one of the treasures of the Hsiung-nu
people. You should not give it away!"

"When a neighboring country asks for it, why should I begrudge
them one horse?" he said, and sent them the thousand-*li* horse.

After a while the Eastern Barbarians, supposing that Mo-tun was
afraid of them, sent an envoy to ask for one of Mo-tun's consorts. Again
Mo-tun questioned his ministers, and they replied in a rage, "The Eastern Barbarians are unreasoning beasts to come and request one of the
Shan'yü's consorts. We beg to attack them!"

But Mo-tun replied, "If it is for a neighboring country, why should
I begrudge them one woman?" and he sent his favorite consort to the
Eastern Barbarians.

With this the ruler of the Eastern Barbarians grew more and more
bold and arrogant, invading the lands to the west. Between his territory
and that of the Hsiung-nu was an area of over a thousand *li* of uninhab-
ited land; the two peoples made their homes on either side of this wasteland.[5] The ruler of the Eastern Barbarians sent an envoy to Mo-tun
saying, "The Hsiung-nu have no way of using this stretch of wasteland

[5] The Gobi Desert. [Translator's note.]

which lies between my border and yours. I would like to take possession of it!"

When Mo-tun consulted his ministers, some of them said, "Since the land is of no use you might as well give it to him," while others said, "No, you must not give it away!"

Mo-tun flew into a rage. "Land is the basis of the nation!" he said. "Why should I give it away?" And he executed all the ministers who had advised him to do so.

Then he mounted his horse and set off to attack the Eastern Barbarians, circulating an order throughout his domain that anyone who was slow to follow would be executed. The Eastern Barbarians had up until this time despised Mo-tun and made no preparations for their defense; when Mo-tun and his soldiers arrived, they inflicted a crushing defeat, killing the ruler of the Eastern Barbarians, taking prisoner his subjects, and seizing their domestic animals. Then he returned and rode west, attacking and routing the Yüeh-chih, and annexed the lands of the ruler of Lou-fan and the ruler of Po-yang south of the Yellow River. Thus he recovered possession of all the lands which the Ch'in general Meng T'ien had taken away from the Hsiung-nu; the border between his territory and that of the Han empire now followed the old line of defenses south of the Yellow River, and from there he marched into the Ch'ao-na and Fu-shih districts and then invaded Yen and Tai.

At this time the Han forces were stalemated in battle with the armies of Hsiang Yü, and China was exhausted by warfare. Thus Mo-tun was able to strengthen his position, massing a force of over three hundred thousand skilled crossbowmen.

Over a thousand years had elapsed from the time of Ch'un-wei, the ancestor of the Hsiung-nu, to that of Mo-tun, a vast period during which the tribes split up and scattered into various groups, sometimes expanding, sometimes dwindling in size. Thus it is impossible to give any ordered account of the Hsiung-nu rulers. When Mo-tun came to power, however, the Hsiung-nu reached their peak of strength and size, subjugating all of the other barbarian tribes of the north and turning south to confront China as an enemy nation. As a result of this, it is possible to give an account here of the later Hsiung-nu rulers and of the offices and titles of the nation.

Under the *Shan-yü* are the Wise Kings of the Left and Right, the left and right Lu-li kings, left and right generals, left and right commandants, left and right household administrators, and left and right Ku-tu marquises. The Hsiung-nu word for "wise" is *"t'u-ch'i,"* so that the heir of the *Shan-yü* is customarily called the *"T'u-ch'i* King of the Left." Among the other leaders, from the wise kings on down to the household administrators, the more important ones command ten thousand horsemen and the lesser ones several thousand, numbering twenty-four leaders in all, though all are known by the title of "Ten Thousand Horsemen." The high ministerial offices are hereditary, being filled from generation to generation by the members of the Hu-yen and Lan families, and in more recent times by the Hsü-pu family. These three families constitute the aristocracy of the nation. The kings and other leaders of the left live in the eastern sector, the region from Shang-ku east to the lands of the Hui-mo and Ch'ao-hsien peoples. The kings and leaders of the right live in the west, the area from Shang Province west to the territories of the Yüeh-chih and Ch'iang tribes. The *Shan-yü* has his court in the region north of Tai and Yün-chung. Each group has its own area, within which it moves about from place to place looking for water and pasture. The Left and Right Wise Kings and Lu-li kings are the most powerful, while the Ku-tu marquises assist the *Shan-yü* in the administration of the nation. Each of the twenty-four leaders in turn appoints his own "chiefs of a thousand," "chiefs of a hundred," and "chiefs of ten," as well as his subordinate kings, prime ministers, chief commandants, household administrators, *chü-ch'ü* officials, and so forth.

In the first month of the year the various leaders come together in a small meeting at the *Shan-yü*'s court to perform sacrifices, and in the fifth month a great meeting is held at Lung-ch'eng at which sacrifices are conducted to the Hsiung-nu ancestors, Heaven and Earth, and the gods and spirits. In the autumn, when the horses are fat, another great meeting is held at the Tai Forest when a reckoning is made of the number of persons and animals.

According to Hsiung-nu law, anyone who in ordinary times draws his sword a foot from the scabbard is condemned to death. Anyone convicted of theft has his property confiscated. Minor offenses are punished by flogging and major ones by death. No one is kept in jail awaiting sentence longer than ten days, and the number of imprisoned men for the whole nation does not exceed a handful.[6]

At dawn the *Shan-yü* leaves his camp and makes obeisance to the sun as it rises, and in the evening he makes a similar obeisance to the moon. In seating arrangements the left side or the seat facing north is considered the place of honor. The days *wu* and *chi* of the ten-day week are regarded as most auspicious.

---

[6] Sima Qian is inviting a comparison with the situation in China in his own day, when the jails were full to overflowing with men awaiting sentence. [Translator's note.]

In burials the Hsiung-nu use an inner and an outer coffin, with accessories of gold, silver, clothing, and fur, but they do not construct grave mounds or plant trees on the grave, nor do they use mourning garments. When a ruler dies, the ministers and concubines who were favored by him and who are obliged to follow him in death often number in the hundreds or even thousands.

Whenever the Hsiung-nu begin some undertaking, they observe the stars and the moon. They attack when the moon is full and withdraw their troops when it wanes. After a battle those who have cut off the heads of the enemy or taken prisoners are presented with a cup of wine and allowed to keep the spoils they have captured. Any prisoners that are taken are made slaves. Therefore, when they fight, each man strives for his own gain. They are very skillful at using decoy troops to lure their opponents to destruction. When they catch sight of the enemy, they swoop down like a flock of birds, eager for booty, but when they find themselves hard pressed and beaten, they scatter and vanish like the mist. Anyone who succeeds in recovering the body of a comrade who has fallen in battle receives all of the dead man's property.

Shortly after the period described above, Mo-tun launched a series of campaigns to the north, conquering the tribes of Hun-yü, Ch'ü-she, Ting-ling, Ko-k'un, and Hsin-li. Thus the nobles and high ministers of the Hsiung-nu were all won over by Mo-tun, considering him a truly worthy leader.

At this time Kao-tsu, the founder of the Han, had just succeeded in winning control of the empire and had transferred Hsin, the former king of Hann, to the rulership of Tai, with his capital at Ma-i. The Hsiung-nu surrounded Ma-i and attacked the city in great force, whereupon Hann Hsin surrendered to them. With Hann Hsin on their side, they then proceeded to lead their troops south across Mount Chü-chu and attack T'ai-yüan, marching as far as the city of Chin-yang. Emperor Kao-tsu led an army in person to attack them, but it was winter and he encountered such cold and heavy snow that two or three out of every ten of his men lost their fingers from frostbite. Mo-tun feigned a retreat to lure the Han soldiers on to an attack. When they came after him in pursuit, he concealed all of his best troops and left only his weakest and puniest men to be observed by the Han scouts. With this the entire Han force, supplemented by three hundred and twenty thousand infantry, rushed north to pursue him; Kao-tsu led the way, advancing as far as the city of P'ing-ch'eng.

Before the infantry had had a chance to arrive, however, Mo-tun swooped down with four hundred thousand of his best cavalry, surrounded Kao-tsu on White Peak, and held him there for seven days. The Han forces within the encirclement had no way of receiving aid or provisions from their comrades outside, since the Hsiung-nu cavalry surrounded them on all sides, with white horses on the west side, greenish horses on the east, black horses on the north, and red ones on the south.[7]

Kao-tsu sent an envoy in secret to Mo-tun's consort, presenting her with generous gifts, whereupon she spoke to Mo-tun, saying, "Why should the rulers of these two nations make such trouble for each other? Even if you gained possession of the Han lands, you could never occupy them. And the ruler of the Han may have his guardian deities as well as you. I beg you to consider the matter well!"

Mo-tun had previously arranged for the troops of Wang Huang and Chao Li, two of Hann Hsin's generals, to meet with him, but though the appointed time had come, they failed to appear and he began to suspect that they were plotting with the Han forces. He therefore decided to listen to his consort's advice and withdrew his forces from one corner of the encirclement. Kao-tsu ordered his men to load their crossbows with arrows and hold them in readiness pointed toward the outside. These preparations completed, they marched straight out of the encirclement and finally joined up with the rest of the army.

Mo-tun eventually withdrew his men and went away, and Kao-tsu likewise retreated and abandoned the campaign, dispatching Liu Ching to conclude a peace treaty with the Hsiung-nu instead.

[7] These four colors are symbolic of the four directions in Chinese belief and, if the narrative is correct, of the Xiongnu belief as well. [Translator's note.]

2

BAN GU

History of the Former Han Dynasty

Late First Century CE

Ban Gu (32–92 CE) was court historian in the Later Han dynasty (25–220 CE), and he compiled the official history of the Former Han dynasty (206 BCE–24 CE) based on imperial archives. He followed Sima Qian's method of compiling data, but restrained the tone of his narrative to adopt a more official style. The following passages are from his biography of Zhang Qian and his description of the Western Regions. Zhang Qian (d. 114 BCE), the envoy of the Han emperor Wudi to the Yuezhi chief, was the first historically recorded Chinese to travel through Mongolia and Central Asia to Da Xia, or Bactria, as the Greeks called it, in northern Afghanistan. Thirteen years later, he returned to the Han court with information about the nomadic tribes and oasis states west of China. His descriptions of the wonders and curiosities of the Western Regions, especially the "heavenly horses," were of great interest to China's commercial communities. What was the most important accomplishment of Zhang Qian's mission?

[Zhang Qian]

Zhang Qian, from Hanzhong, was serving as a royal attendant during the Jianyuan era.[1] At that time, defectors from the Xiongnu brought information that the Xiongnu had defeated the Yuezhi and had made the Yuezhi king's skull into a ritual drinking vessel. The Yuezhi people had retreated, hating the Xiongnu, but could not find an ally to help them take revenge. The Han court was just getting ready to attack the Xiongnu when this bad news arrived. The emperor then decided to send an envoy to the Yuezhi court. Knowing that this would be a dangerous

[1] Hanzhong is in present-day Shaanxi Province; the dates of the Jianyuan era are 140–135 BCE.

Ban Gu, *Han Shu* [History of the Former Han Dynasty] (Beijing: Zhonghua Shuju, 1962), 61:2687; 96a:3894–95. Translated by Xinru Liu.

mission because the envoy would have to pass through the territory of the Xiongnu before he could make contact with the Yuezhi, the emperor asked for volunteers. Zhang Qian, a low-level courtier, answered the call and became the imperial envoy. His companion on the trip was Gan Fu, a slave of the Tangyi family. They exited Han territory through Longxi.[2] Unfortunately, Xiongnu tribesmen caught them and sent them to the court of the Shanyu, who was their chief. The Shanyu said, "The Yuezhi are located to the north of my territory, so how can the Han send an envoy to them? If I wanted to send an envoy to the Yue,[3] would the Han court let me pass through their territory to get there?" He detained Zhang Qian for more than a decade, during which time he also provided him with a Xiongnu wife who bore him a son. Zhang, however, always kept the emblem that identified him as a Han envoy and never forgot his mission.

Eventually, when Zhang Qian was living on the western frontier of the Xiongnu domain, he got an opportunity to escape and headed west toward the Yuezhi, along with his retinue. After walking several dozen days, they arrived at Dayuan.[4] The king of Dayuan had heard about the wealth of the Han Chinese and was willing to have talks and establish trade with them. Thus, delighted to see an envoy from the Han, he asked about Zhang's mission. Zhang told him, "I was sent out as an envoy to the Yuezhi, but I was blocked by the Xiongnu. Now I am free from the Xiongnu. If your majesty provides me with a guide to help me find the Yuezhi, once I have returned to the Han court, the Han emperor will grant you countless gifts." The king of Dayuan believed him and sent him a guide and interpreter who would travel with him to Kangju.[5] The Kangju people then helped them reach the court of the Great Yuezhi. After the king of the Great Yuezhi had been killed by the Xiongnu, his wife had become the chief of the tribe. The Yuezhi had then conquered Da Xia[6] and ruled that state where the land was fertile and peaceful. The Yuezhi people enjoyed life there very much and felt that China was too far away to be a useful ally, and they knew that it was not in their best interest to try to avenge the wrongs done to them by attacking the Xiongnu. Thus, when Zhang visited the Yuezhi court in Bactria, he could not persuade their chief to ally with the Han and attack the Xiongnu.

[2] In present-day Gansu Province.
[3] Tribes in southeastern China.
[4] Ferghana, in present-day Uzbekistan.
[5] Sogdiana, in present-day Uzbekistan, west of Dayuan.
[6] Bactria, in present-day northern Afghanistan.

After living more than a year with the Yuezhi, Zhang left Bactria and started on the trip back home to China. He tried to follow the routes through the mountains that would take him to Qiang[7] in order to avoid the Xiongnu, but that plan did not work, and again he was caught by the Xiongnu. A year later, the Shanyu's death was followed by a civil war. Taking advantage of this opportunity, Zhang escaped, together with his Xiongnu wife and children as well as Gan Fu, and they then eventually returned to the Han court in Chang'an. Zhang was honored with the title of Grand Minister, and Gan Fu received the title of Companion of the Envoy.

Zhang was energetic and steadfast, as well as generous and tolerant, and thus the barbarians all loved him. Gan Fu was a native of the steppe and a good archer. When they ran out of food, Gan Fu shot birds and other animals to feed the group. Zhang Qian had left Chang'an with a retinue of one hundred. Thirteen years later, he came back with only Gan Fu.

Zhang Qian visited Dayuan, Great Yuezhi, Da Xia, and Kangju, and he had heard about five or six other major states in that area. He described all the geographic features and the products of all the countries. These details are recorded in the chapter on the Western Regions in this book.

[The Western Regions]

The king of Dayuan ruled from the city of Guishan, which is about 12,500 *li*[8] from Chang'an. It has sixty thousand households, with a population of three hundred thousand (which includes the sixty thousand soldiers among them). A viceroy and a prime minister assist the king. Some 4,031 li east of it is the headquarters of the Han Protectorate established in the Western Region; 1,510 li north of it is the Beitian city of Kangju; 690 li southwest of it is where the Great Yuezhi are located. It thus borders Kangju to its north and the Great Yuezhi to its south. Its geography, customs, and products are similar to those of the Great Yuezhi and the Parthians. Dayuan and its surrounding region make wine from grapes. Rich households store as many as 10,000 *shi*.[9] The wine is stored so well that it maintains its quality for several decades. People there love drinking wine, and the horses there like alfalfa.

---

[7] Present-day Qinghai.

[8] During the Han dynasty, one *li* was about one-third of a kilometer, or one-fifth of a mile. The numbers here seem exaggerated.

[9] During the Han dynasty, one *shi* was the equivalent of forty-one liters today.

There are more than seventy cities other than the capital in Dayuan. There are many excellent horses, which sweat blood.[10] It is said that the horses are descendants of the heavenly horses.

Zhang Qian once advised the emperor Wudi to get horses from Dayuan. An envoy carrying a thousand units of gold and a golden horse tried to purchase these good horses from Dayuan. The king there thought that the Han court was too far away to send very many troops to his land, and he loved his horses too much to give them away. The Han envoy then reprimanded the king, and the king killed the envoy and took possession of the gifts that the Han emperor had sent. The Son of Heaven[11] sent General Li Guangli to punish Dayuan. The campaign took four years, and more than ten thousand soldiers were involved. The people of Dayuan killed their own king Mugua and surrendered his head, as well as three thousand horses to appease the Han. Only then did the troops of the military expedition turn around and go home.

[10] Some modern scholars believe that the blood-sweating horses must have been sick. During the Han dynasty, the Chinese (and presumably the horses' breeders) did not see this phenomenon as a problem. They called them "heavenly horses," and there was never any question about the quality of the Dayuan horses.
[11] The Han emperor.

3

Documents Excavated from Juyan Fort on the Great Wall

ca. 103 BCE–40 CE

After Emperor Wudi ascended the throne in 140 BCE, the Han dynasty built the Juyan Fort on the Great Wall in modern Gansu Province. Here soldiers were stationed in watchtowers to guard against nomadic invasions. In time, they were encouraged to settle there and farm so that the garrison communities could be self-sustaining. The soldiers' daily lives are known to us through notes they made on wooden slips deposited inside the watchtowers and discovered during an archaeological survey sponsored by

Chen Zhi, *Juyan Hanjian Yanjiu* [Studies of the Wooden Slips from Juyan] (Tianjin: Guji Chubanshe, 1986), 492–93, 204, 205, 327–29. Translated by Xinru Liu.

the Chinese government in 1930–1931. The following selection includes a letter from a Chinese officer of low rank to his wife, two passports or travelers' documents of the kind examined by the soldiers on duty, and lists of work assignments that indicate how tasks were allocated among the soldiers and what work was necessary to maintain irrigation systems, repair tools, cook food, and take care of horses on the frontier. The letter was written in classical Chinese and followed the writing customs of the time, though its composition and calligraphy are poor. What do these documents reveal about the life of a soldier on the Great Wall and about the reasons travelers requested permission to go outside the gates? What do they suggest about the Han dynasty's control of its subjects?

Letter from an Officer to His Wife

Xuan[1] *prostrate to pay respect:*

Yousun,[2] my dear wife, your life is really hard. Being at the frontier in the summer, I hope you have enough food and clothing. If this is true, I feel happy at the frontier. Only because of the support of Yousun, Xuan can serve at the frontier faithfully, and have no need to worry about home.

Your brother Youdu followed the county governor to arrive at Juyan on the tenth day of the [?] month. He told me that your parents were fine. As he came here for business in a great hurry, he probably did not get a chance to see you before his departure.

. . . On the eleventh day, I came here to report to Houguan.[3] As the work is not finished yet, I take time to write this letter, wish all my best.

XUAN

PS

Yousun my dear wife:

I just received a letter from Zhu Youji, saying the station chief has arrived at the Linqu watchtower. I am writing this letter to you Yousun. The Houguan will be gone tomorrow. The inspector has not arrived yet. I had better work hard now so that I will not receive a low grade of assessment among the officers when inspected.

---

[1] Name the officer called himself.
[2] Name of the officer's wife.
[3] Title of Xuan's superior officer.

Travelers' Passports

1

The fifth year of the Yongshi era,[4] the day of Jisi, the first day of the month, the hour of Bingzi, Zhong, the Officer of Beixiang, reports the following: Cui Zidang, a man from the neighborhood of Yichengli, applies for a passport to travel to Juyan for family business. The man has no criminal record; therefore he should be cleared for passing Shuijin Gate and Suo Gate in Juyan County. Thus I report.

In the leap month, the day of Bingzi, Peng, the Deputy Magistrate of Lude County, approves [Cui's] passing of Shuijin Gate and Suo Gate in Juyan County, according to the statute and decree.

[Signed By]
YAN, Subordinate official
JIAN, the Scribe

2

The second year of the Yuanyan era,[5] the tenth month, the day of Yiyou, Shang, the Magistrate of the county, and Zhong, the Deputy Magistrate, issued the passport for counties, roads, waterways and fords, and gates for Wang Feng, the Police Chief. Wang is going to purchase horses ordered by the court of emperor in Jiuquan, Dunhuang, and Zhangye Prefectures. Guest house staff and managers should follow the order according to the statute and decree.

[Signed By]
YI, Scribe of [?]
BAO, Assistant

Soldiers' Work Assignments

1

The Eleventh Month, Day Dingsi,
Twenty-four soldiers:
One is the chief.
Three cook food.
One is sick.
Two bind up reeds.

---

[4] 12 BCE, in the leap month of the lunar calendar.
[5] 11 BCE.

Therefore, seven are not in the main workforce.
Ten people harvest reeds five hundred. . . .
. . . arrow makers cut thirty [?], making 5,520 arrows.

2

The Eighth Month, Day Jiachen
Twenty-nine soldiers:
One is the chief.
Three cook food for soldiers.
. . . four people . . .
Twenty-five are in the main workforce.
Two cut wood.
Six collect fodder.
Fourteen transport fodder in the quantity of 4,020 bundles.
[Other soldiers] do the 290. . . .
Two make horse gears. . . .

3

Ten soldiers: . . .
One guards the garden.
One hoes the garden soil.
One runs errands.
One collects dog feces.
One cooks food for officers.
Two walk the horses.
One carves bows.

2

Rome's Trade to the East, First Century BCE–Second Century CE

4

STRABO

The Geography

Early First Century CE

Some three hundred years after Alexander's Central Asian conquests, Strabo (ca. 63 BCE–24 CE), a Greek geographer who lived in the time of the Roman emperor Augustus, traveled extensively to collect information about the conquered lands for his famous geography. He also took advantage of earlier Greek writers and information from traders. His descriptions of Bactria and Sogdiana contain some reliable information, but also much that is fanciful. Like Arrian (Document 5), he records Alexander's strategies of conquest. The Greeks found it interesting that well-established city-dwellers in Central Asia were closely affiliated with the nomads and shared many cultural traits with them. Strabo's descriptions of "barbaric" customs also have been of interest to modern historians. For instance, Sogdians' use of dogs as "undertakers" to dispose of dead bodies indicates that they followed a type of Zoroastrian funeral rite. This information, although strange, is not false, but it is difficult for a scholar from a different culture to understand. Now that the Romans had commercial contacts with Central Asia, how well do you think they understood the cultures of their trading partners?

Strabo, *The Geography of Strabo*, trans. Horace Leonard Jones (Cambridge, Mass.: Harvard University Press, 1928), 5:279–87.

51

As for Bactria, a part of it lies alongside Aria towards the north, though most of it lies above Aria and to the east of it. And much of it produces everything except oil. The Greeks who caused Bactria to revolt grew so powerful on account of the fertility of the country that they became masters, not only of Ariana, but also of India, as Apollodorus of Artemita says: and more tribes were subdued by them than by Alexander—by Menander[1] in particular (at least if he actually crossed the Hypanis towards the east and advanced as far as the Imaüs), for some were subdued by him personally and others by Demetrius, the son of Euthydemus the king of the Bactrians; and they took possession, not only of Patalena, but also, on the rest of the coast, of what is called the kingdom of Saraostus and Sigerdis. In short, Apollodorus says that Bactriana is the ornament of Ariana as a whole; and, more than that, they extended their empire even as far as the Seres[2] and the Phryni.

Their cities were Bactra (also called Zariaspa, through which flows a river bearing the same name and emptying into the Oxus), and Darapsa, and several others. Among these was Eucratidia, which was named after its ruler. The Greeks took possession of it and divided it into satrapies, of which the satrapy Turiva and that of Aspionus were taken away from Eucratides by the Parthians. And they also held Sogdiana, situated above Bactriana towards the east between the Oxus River, which forms the boundary between the Bactrians and the Sogdians, and the Iaxartes River. And the Iaxartes forms also the boundary between the Sogdians and the nomads.

Now in early times the Sogdians and Bactrians did not differ much from the nomads in their modes of life and customs, although the Bactrians were a little more civilised; however, of these, as of the others, Onesicritus does not report their best traits, saying, for instance, that those who have become helpless because of old age or sickness are thrown out alive as prey to dogs kept expressly for this purpose, which in their native tongue are called "undertakers," and that while the land outside the walls of the metropolis of the Bactrians looks clean, yet most of the land inside the walls is full of human bones; but that Alexander broke up the custom. And the reports about the Caspians are similar, for instance, that when parents live beyond seventy years they are shut in and starved to death. Now this latter custom is more tolerable; and it is similar to that of the Ceians, although it is of Scythian origin: that of the Bactrians, however, is much more like that of Scythians. And so, if

---

[1] Menander, known in Buddhist literature as Milinda, was a Greek king who ruled northwestern India in the late second century BCE.
[2] Seres, "land of silk," was the Greek and Roman name for China.

it was proper to be in doubt as to the facts at the time when Alexander was finding such customs there, what should one say as to what sort of customs were probably in vogue among them in the time of the earliest Persian rulers and the still earlier rulers?

Be this as it may, they say that Alexander founded eight cities in Bactriana and Sogdiana, and that he rased certain cities to the ground, among which was Cariatae in Bactriana, in which Callisthenes was seized and imprisoned, and Maracanda and Cyra in Sogdiana, Cyra being the last city founded by Cyrus[3] and being situated on the Iaxartes River, which was the boundary of the Persian empire; and that although this settlement was fond of Cyrus, he rased it to the ground because of its frequent revolts; and that through a betrayal he took also two strongly fortified rocks, one in Bactriana, that of Sisimithres, where Oxyartes kept his daughter Rhoxana, and the other in Sogdiana, that of Oxus, though some call it the rock of Ariamazes. Now writers report that that of Sisimithres is fifteen stadia in height and eighty in circuit, and that on top it is level and has a fertile soil which can support five hundred men, and that here Alexander met with sumptuous hospitality and married Rhoxana, the daughter of Oxyartes; but the rock in Sogdiana, they say, is twice as high as that in Bactriana. And near these places, they say, Alexander destroyed also the city of the Branchidae, whom Xerxes[4] had settled there—people who voluntarily accompanied him from their home-land—because of the fact that they had betrayed to him the riches and treasures of the god at Didyma. Alexander destroyed the city, they add, because he abominated the sacrilege and the betrayal.

Aristobulus calls the river which flows through Sogdiana Polytimetus, a name imposed by the Macedonians (just as they imposed names on many other places, giving new names to some and slightly altering the spelling of the names of others); and watering the country it empties into a desert and sandy land, and is absorbed in the sand, like the Arius which flows through the country of the Arians. It is said that people digging near the Ochus River found a spring of oil. It is reasonable to suppose that, just as nitrous and astringent and bituminous and sulphurous liquids flow through the earth, so also oily liquids are found; but the rarity causes surprise.[5] According to some, the Ochus flows through Bactriana; according to others, alongside it. And according to some, it is a different river from the Oxus as far as its mouths, being more to the south than the Oxus, although they both have their outlets into the Caspian Sea in

---

[3] Cyrus (d. 529 BCE) was the founder of the Achaemenid Empire in Persia.
[4] Xerxes (ca. 519–465 BCE) was a Persian king best known to the Greek world for his defeat at the naval battle at Salamis.
[5] Refers to petroleum.

Hyrcania, whereas others say that it is different at first, but unites with the Oxus, being in many places as much as six or seven stadia wide. The Iaxartes, however, from beginning to end, is a different river from the Oxus, and although it ends in the same sea, the mouths of the two, according to Patrocles, are about eighty parasangs distant from one another. The Persian parasang, according to some, is sixty stadia, but according to others thirty or forty. When I was sailing up the Nile, they used different measures when they named the distance in "schoeni" from city to city, so that in some places the same number of "schoeni" meant a longer voyage and in others a shorter; and thus the variations have been preserved to this day as handed down from the beginning.

Now the tribes one encounters in going from Hyrcania towards the rising sun as far as Sogdiana became known at first to the Persians—I mean the tribes inside Taurus—and afterwards to the Macedonians and to the Parthians; and the tribes situated on the far side of those tribes and in a straight line with them are supposed, from their identity in kind, to be Scythian, although no expeditions have been made against them that I know of, any more than against the most northerly of the nomads. Now Alexander did attempt to lead an expedition against these when he was in pursuit of Bessus and Spitamenes, but when Bessus was captured alive and brought back, and Spitamenes was slain by the barbarians, he desisted from his undertaking. It is not generally agreed that persons have sailed around from India to Hyrcania, but Patrocles states that it is possible.

5

ARRIAN

The Campaigns of Alexander

ca. 145–160 CE

Arrian (ca. 86–160 CE) was a Greek scholar who served in the Roman Empire as a military commander and administrator. After retiring from imperial politics, he settled in Athens around 145 CE to pursue the life of a scholar and to study accounts of Alexander in preparation for writing

Arrian, *The Campaigns of Alexander*, trans. Aubrey de Sélincourt (Harmondsworth, U.K.: Penguin Books, 1971), 205–10, 227–29.

his own. He deemed the account of Ptolemy, one of Alexander's generals and later a king of Egypt, to be the most reliable, but he also used the account of Aristobulus, an engineer contemporary of Alexander known for his keen observation of geography and nature. The following passages describe Alexander's encounters with nomadic peoples in Central Asia. The Greeks referred to all these nomads as Scythians, but they apparently came from different communities and places and held different attitudes toward the Greeks. Look for the variety of strategies the nomads developed for dealing with this powerful newcomer, as well as for Alexander's strategies of conquest.

[Alexander and the Asian Scythians]

About this time a force of Asian Scythians arrived at the Tanais. Most of them had heard that some of the tribes beyond the river had declared their hostility to Alexander and intended to join in an attack upon the Macedonians in the event of a serious rising. A report also came in that Spitamenes was blockading the troops which had been left behind in the fortress of Marakanda. To meet this situation, Andromachus, Menedemus, and Caranus were dispatched with a force consisting of sixty Companions, 800 of Caranus' mercenaries, and some 1,500 mercenary infantry. Pharnuches the interpreter was attached to the troops: he was a Lycian, thoroughly familiar with the language of this part of the country, and had often shown a skilful touch in dealing with the natives.

Alexander spent twenty days on the work of fortifying the site of his proposed new town and arranging for the settlement there of any Greek mercenaries and neighbouring tribesmen who expressed a wish to avail themselves of the opportunity, and also of a number of Macedonians no longer fit for active service. To mark the occasion, after his customary religious observances he held games, with athletic and equestrian contests.

Meanwhile the Scythians made no move to leave the Tanais. The river was not broad at that point; they could be seen shooting arrows into the water, and heard calling out, in their barbarous way, insulting remarks to Alexander and boasting that he would never dare to lay a finger upon men like them—or, if he did, that he would soon find out the difference between Scythians and Asiatic savages. To Alexander such an exhibition was most annoying, so he proposed to cross the river and deal with them as they deserved. The skin floats were being prepared for the crossing when he found that the omens, at the preliminary sacrifice, were against him. In spite of his vexation, he nevertheless made the best of it and abandoned the enterprise. The Scythians, however, continuing their insufferable behaviour, he sacrificed again; but this time, too, Aristander the seer declared that the omens portended danger. Thereupon Alexander replied that it was better to face the worst of perils than for the conqueror of nearly all Asia to make himself ridiculous to a pack of Scythians—as Darius, the father of Xerxes, had done long ago. None the less, Aristander refused to misinterpret the divine prediction merely because Alexander wished it otherwise.

When all the skin floats were ready and the army in full equipment drawn up on the river-bank, the catapults, at the word of command, opened up on the Scythians who were riding along the edge of the water on the further side. Some of them were hit; one was pierced through both shield and breastplate and fell dead from his horse. The Scythians were taken completely aback by the long range of the catapults, and that, together with the loss of a good man, induced them to withdraw a short distance from the river, whereupon Alexander, seeing their consternation, ordered the trumpets to sound and himself led the way over the water, followed by his men. First to be put ashore were the archers and slingers, who were then ordered to open up on the enemy to prevent them from closing on the main infantry units before the mounted troops were all safely over; then as soon as every man was across and the army massed on the river-bank, a regiment of mercenaries and four squadrons of lancers were ordered forward to lead the attack. The Scythians met the challenge; their numbers were for the moment superior; they made circles round the small attacking force, shooting as they rode, and then galloped off to a safe distance. At this Alexander ordered an advance by a mixed force consisting of the cavalry together with the archers, the Agrianes, and the other light troops under Balacrus, and, when they were almost within striking distance, gave the word for three regiments of the Companions and all the mounted javelin-men to charge, while he himself at the head of the remaining cavalry came on at the gallop with his squadrons in column.

This effectually put a stop to the enemy's circling movements; the Macedonian cavalry, with the light troops mixed with it in close support, was now right on top of them, and it was no longer possible for them to repeat their former manœuvre without the certainty of destruction. Indeed, from this moment they were well and truly beaten; in their attempt to get away, about 1,000 were killed, including Satraces, one of their commanders, and some 150 were made prisoner.

The rapid pursuit, in the great heat, was exhausting; every man suffered acutely from thirst, and Alexander himself, as he rode, was forced to drink whatever water he could find. Unfortunately it was not pure, and gave him a severe attack of dysentery. This proved the salvation of some, at any rate, of the Scythians; for had not Alexander had this trouble, I do not think a single one of them would have escaped with his life.

Alexander did, in fact, become very seriously ill, and was carried back to camp—so Aristander was a true prophet after all. . . .

[Alexander and the European Scythians]

Alexander was now for the second time visited by envoys from the European Scythians, who arrived in company with the envoys he had himself sent to Scythia. The reigning King of Scythia at the time of their dispatch had died; he had been succeeded by his brother, and the purpose of the present embassy was to express the willingness of Scythia to accede in every point to Alexander's instructions; they brought as presents from the King such things as are reckoned most valuable in their country, and communicated to Alexander their King's desire to cement the friendship and alliance between their countries by giving him his daughter in marriage. Should Alexander be unwilling to marry the Scythian Princess, the King was none the less anxious to do the next best thing and to give as brides to his most trusted officers the daughters of the governors and other personages of rank in Scythian territory. He would, moreover, visit Alexander in person, if he were called upon to do so, and thus be enabled to take his instructions from Alexander's own lips.

About the same time the King of the Chorasmians, Pharasmanes, arrived at the Court with 1,500 mounted troops.[1] He told Alexander that his territory had common frontiers with the Colchians and the Amazon women,[2] and that if Alexander should ever contemplate an invasion of those countries with the object of reducing the various peoples in that part of the world as far as the Black Sea, he was willing to act as his guide and to provide all the necessary supplies for his army.

To the envoys from Scythia, Alexander gave a polite and suitable reply: he had no need, he said, of a Scythian marriage. He thanked Pharasmanes for his offer and concluded a pact of friendship with him, adding that an expedition to the Black Sea was not at the moment convenient; and, before dismissing him, he put him in touch with Artabazus, the Persian, to whom he had given charge of affairs in Bactria, and

[1] The Chorasmians inhabited the country (Khiva) between the Caspian and Aral Seas. [Translator's note.]

[2] Valiant women of a matriarchal nation in Greek mythology. Here Alexander could have been encountering a matriarchal community in Central Asia.

also with the various governors of the neighbouring provinces. His own thoughts were at present occupied with India, and he pointed out that once India was his he would be master of all Asia, after which his intention was to return to Greece and to make from thence an expedition to the Black Sea region by way of the Hellespont and the Propontis with all his land and sea forces combined. Pharasmanes, therefore, would oblige him if he deferred the fulfilment of his offer until that occasion should arise.

Alexander now returned to the Oxus. His intention was to proceed to Sogdiana, as a report had come in that many of the people there were refusing to obey the governor he had appointed and had shut themselves up in the forts. While he was in camp on the Oxus, a spring of water and another of oil quite near it came up from the ground close to his tent. Ptolemy, son of Lagus, was informed of this remarkable event, and Ptolemy told Alexander, who, to mark his sense of its miraculous nature, offered sacrifice according to the form prescribed by his soothsayers. Aristander declared that the spring of oil was a sign of difficulties to come and of eventual victory.[3]

Four officers—Polysperchon, Attalus, Gorgias, and Meleager—were left in Bactria with instructions to destroy all natives who had refused submission and to keep a sharp look-out for any further trouble; and Alexander himself, after crossing into Sogdiana, divided his remaining strength into five, one division to be commanded by Hephaestion, another by Ptolemy, son of Lagus, a third by Perdiccas, a fourth by Coenus and Artabazus. The fifth he took over himself and proceeded with it in the direction of Marakanda, while the other four commanders carried out offensive operations as opportunity offered, storming the forts where some of the native tribesmen were trying to hold out, or receiving the voluntary surrender of others.

The greater part of Sogdiana was covered by these operations, and when the whole force was reunited at Marakanda, Alexander sent Hephaestion to plant settlements in the various towns, and at the same time dispatched Coenus and Artabazus to Scythia, where Spitamenes, according to report, had taken refuge. Meanwhile Alexander with the remainder of his force marched against those parts of Sogdiana which were still in rebel hands, and had no difficulty in subduing them.

Spitamenes, while all this was going on, had made his way with a number of fugitives from Sogdiana to that branch of the Scythian people

---

[3] The first mention of petroleum in Greek literature. [Translator's note.]

known as the Massagetae;[4] there they got together 600 native horse-men and presented themselves at one of the forts in Bactria. Neither the garrison nor its commander had expected any hostile move; Spitamenes took them by surprise, killed the men, and captured their officer, whom he kept under guard. This success emboldened him a few days later to approach Zariaspa. They did not venture an assault upon the town, though they rounded up a lot of livestock and carried it off as booty.

[4] The Massagetae were a Scythian tribe, living east of the Caspian Sea, who had defeated and killed Cyrus the Great. [Translator's note.]

6

PLINY

Natural History

77 CE

Pliny the Elder (ca. 23–79 CE) was by far the most famous scholar of natural science in the Roman world. For his accounts of the many lands far to the east of Greece, he gathered information from Greek writers of earlier times and from Hellenistic writers of his own time. He was interested in all the products of the East and tried to explain their origins and manufacturing processes. Obviously, his account of silk from distant China is far less accurate than his account of frankincense and myrrh or of purple dye, which he describes in great detail. As a scholar of natural history, Pliny observed the life cycles and environments of the purple murex. He also described the fashions of the Roman elite and their desire to display their wealth through collections of gems. His Natural History, *an encyclopedia of natural science, provides much information about Rome's trade in goods from Arabia, India, and China. What is Pliny's attitude toward the Chinese and toward Chinese and other luxuries in Rome? How does his curiosity about nature reflect the Roman market for the Silk Roads trade?*

[Chinese Silks]

After leaving the Caspian Sea and the Scythian Ocean our course takes a bend towards the Eastern Sea as the coast turns to face eastward. The first part of the coast after the Scythian promontory is uninhabitable on account of snow, and the neighbouring region is uncultivated because of the savagery of the tribes that inhabit it. This is the country of the Cannibal Scythians who eat human bodies; consequently the adjacent districts are waste deserts thronging with wild beasts lying in wait for human beings as savage as themselves. Then we come to more Scythians and to more deserts inhabited by wild beasts, until we reach a mountain range called Tabis which forms a cliff over the sea; and not until we have covered nearly half of the length of the coast that faces north-east is that region inhabited. The first human occupants are the people called the Chinese, who are famous for the woollen substance[1] obtained from their forests; after a soaking in water they comb off the white down of the leaves, and so supply our women with the double task of unravelling the threads and weaving them together again; so manifold is the labour employed, and so distant is the region of the globe drawn upon, to enable the Roman matron to flaunt transparent raiment in public. The Chinese, though mild in character, yet resemble wild animals, in that they also shun the company of the remainder of mankind, and wait for trade to come to them. . . .

[Ebony]

We have already described the wool-bearing trees of the Chinese in making mention of that race, and we have spoken of the large size of the trees in India. One of those peculiar to India, the ebony, is spoken of in glowing terms by Virgil,[2] who states that it does not grow in any other country. Herodotus, however, prefers it to be ascribed to Ethiopia, stating that the Ethiopians used to pay as tribute to the Kings of Persia

---

[1] The "woollen substance" from the Chinese could be silk.
[2] Virgil (70–19 BCE), a Roman poet, is most famous for his epic poem the *Aeneid.*

every three years a hundred logs of ebony, together with gold and ivory. Nor also should we omit the fact, since that author indicates it, that the Ethiopians used to pay twenty large elephant tusks on the same account. So high was the esteem in which ivory was held in the 310th year of our city, the date at which that author composed his history at Thurii in Italy; which makes all the more surprising the statement which we accept on his authority, that nobody of Asia or Greece had hitherto been seen who had ever seen the river Po. The exploration of the geography of Ethiopia, which as we have said had lately been reported to the Emperor Nero,[3] showed that over a space of 1,996 miles from Syene on the frontier of the empire to Meroe trees are rare, and there are none except of the palm species. That is possibly the reason why ebony was the third most important item in the tribute paid. . . .

[Indian Cotton]

In the same gulf is the island of Tyros, which is covered with forests in the part facing east, where it also is flooded by the sea at high tide. Each of the trees is the size of a fig-tree; they have a flower with an indescribably sweet scent and the fruit resembles a lupine, and is so prickly that no animal can touch it. On a more elevated plateau in the same island there are trees that bear wool,[4] but in a different manner to those of the Chinese, as the leaves of these trees have no growth on them, and might be thought to be vine-leaves were it not that they are smaller; but they bear gourds of the size of a quince, which when they ripen burst open and disclose balls of down from which an expensive linen for clothing is made.

Their name for this tree is the gossypinus; it also grows in greater abundance on the smaller island of Tyros, which is ten miles distant from the other. Juba[5] says that this shrub has a woolly down growing round it, the fabric made from which is superior to the linen of India. He also says that there is an Arabian tree called the cynas from which cloth is made, which has foliage resembling a palm-leaf. Similarly the natives of India are provided with clothes by their own trees. But in the Tyros islands there is also another tree with a blossom like a white violet but four times as large; it has no scent, which may well surprise us in that region of the world. . . .

---

[3] Nero (37–68 CE) was a Roman emperor (r. 54–68) whose cruelty provoked widespread rebellions, which led to his suicide.

[4] This wool-bearing tree could be kapok, a tropical tree producing cotton-like fiber.

[5] Juba, king of Mauretania, was respected by Pliny for his knowledge, and Pliny frequently quoted him in the *Natural History*.

[Spices, Frankincense, and Myrrh]

Resembling these substances both in name and in the shrub that produces it is cardamomum, the seeds of which are oblong in shape. It is gathered in Arabia, in the same manner as amomum. It has four varieties: one very green and oily, with sharp corners and awkward to crumble—this is the kind most highly spoken of—the next sort a whitish red, the third shorter and of a colour nearer black, while an inferior kind is mottled and easily friable, and has little scent—in the true kind the scent ought to be near to that of costus. Cardamomum also grows in the country of the Medes. The price of the best sort is 3 denarii a pound.

Next in affinity to cardamomum would have come cinnamomum,[6] were it not convenient first to catalogue the riches of Arabia and the reasons that have given it the names of Happy and Blessed. The chief products of Arabia then are frankincense and myrrh; the latter it shares also with the Cave-dwellers' Country, but no country beside Arabia produces frankincense, and not even the whole of Arabia. About in the middle of that country are the Astramitae, a district of the Sabaei, the capital of their realm being Sabota, situated on a lofty mountain; and eight days' journey from Sabota is a frankincense-producing district belonging to the Sabaei called Sariba—according to the Greeks the name means "secret mystery." The region faces north-east, and is surrounded by impenetrable rocks, and on the right hand side bordered by a seacoast with inaccessible cliffs. The soil is reported to be of a milky white colour with a tinge of red. The forests measure 20 *schoeni* in length and half that distance in breadth—by the calculation of Eratosthenes a *schoenus* measures 40 furlongs, that is five miles, but some authorities have made the *schoenus* 32 furlongs. There are hills rising to a great height, with natural forests on them running right down to the level ground. It is generally agreed that the soil is clay, and that there are few springs and these charged with alkali. Adjacent to the Astramitae is another district, the Minaei, through whose territory the transit for the export of the frankincense is along one narrow track. It was these people who originated the trade and who chiefly practise it, and from them the perfume takes the name of "Minaean"; none of the Arabs beside these have ever seen an incense-tree, and not even all of these, and it is said that there are not more than 3000 families who retain the right of trading in it as a hereditary property, and that consequently the members of these families are called sacred and are not allowed to be polluted by ever meeting women or funeral processions when they are engaged in making incisions in the trees in order to obtain the frankincense, and that

---

[6] Cinnamon. Both cardamom and cinnamon likely came from India in the time of Pliny.

in this way the price of the commodity is increased owing to scruples of religion. Some persons report that the frankincense in the forests belongs to all these peoples in common, but others state that it is shared out among them in yearly turns.

Nor is there agreement in regard to the appearance of the incense-tree itself. We have carried on operations in Arabia, and the arms of Rome have penetrated into a large part of it; indeed, Gaius Caesar, son of Augustus,[7] won great renown from the country; yet no Latin writer, so far as I know, has described the appearance of this tree. The descriptions given by the Greeks vary: some have stated that it has the leaf of a pear-tree, only smaller and of a grass-green colour; others that it resembles the mastich and has a reddish leaf; some that it is a kind of terebinth, and that this was the view of King Antigonus, to whom a plant was brought. King Juba in his volumes dedicated to Gaius Caesar, son of Augustus, whose imagination was fired by the fame of Arabia, states that the tree has a twisted stem and branches closely resembling those of the Pontic maple and that it gives a juice like that of the almond; he says that trees of this description are to be seen in Carmania and in Egypt, where they were introduced under the influence of the Ptolemies when they reigned there. It is well known that it has the bark of a bay-tree, and some have said that the leaf is also like that of the bay; at all events that was the case with the tree when it was grown at Sardis—for the Kings of Asia also interested themselves in planting it. The ambassadors who have come to Rome from Arabia in my time have made all these matters still more uncertain, which may well surprise us, seeing that even some sprigs of the incense-tree find their way to Rome, on the evidence of which we may believe that the parent tree also is smooth and tapering and that it puts out its shoots from a trunk that is free from knots.

It used to be the custom, when there were fewer opportunities of selling frankincense, to gather it only once a year, but at the present day trade introduces a second harvesting. The earlier and natural gathering takes place at about the rising of the Dog-star,[8] when the summer heat is most intense. They make an incision where the bark appears to be fullest of juice and distended to its thinnest; and the bark is loosened with a blow, but not removed. From the incision a greasy foam spurts out, which coagulates and thickens, being received on a mat of palm-leaves where the nature of the ground requires this, but in other places

---

[7] Augustus (63 BCE–14 CE) was the first emperor of the Roman Empire (r. 27 BCE–14 CE).

[8] A popular name for Sirius, the most brilliant star in the sky, which lies in the constellation Canis Major, the Great Dog. The rising of the Dog-star coincides with the beginning of summer.

on a space round the tree that has been rammed hard. The frankincense collected in the latter way is in a purer state, but the former method produces a heavier weight; while the residue adhering to the tree is scraped off with an iron tool, and consequently contains fragments of bark. The forest is divided up into definite portions, and owing to the mutual honesty of the owners is free from trespassing, and though nobody keeps guard over the trees after an incision has been made, nobody steals from his neighbour. At Alexandria, on the other hand, where the frankincense is worked up for sale, good heavens! no vigilance is sufficient to guard the factories. A seal is put upon the workmen's aprons, they have to wear a mask or a net with a close mesh on their heads, and before they are allowed to leave the premises they have to take off all their clothes: so much less honesty is displayed with regard to the produce with them than as to the forests with the growers. The frankincense from the summer crop is collected in autumn; this is the purest kind, bright white in colour. The second crop is harvested in the spring, cuts having been made in the bark during the winter in preparation for it; the juice that comes out on this occasion is reddish, and not to be compared with the former taking, the name for which is carfiathum, the other being called dathiathum. Also the juice produced by a sapling is believed to be whiter, but that from an older tree has more scent. Some people also think that a better kind is produced on islands, but Juba says that no incense grows on islands at all.

Frankincense that hangs suspended in a globular drop we call male frankincense, although in other connexions the term "male" is not usually employed where there is no female; but it is said to have been due to religious scruple that the name of the other sex was not employed in this case. Some people think that male frankincense is so called from its resemblance to the testes. The frankincense most esteemed, however, is the breast-shaped, formed when, while a previous drop is still hanging suspended, another one following unites with it. I find it recorded that one of these lumps used to be a whole handful, in the days when men's eagerness to pluck them was less greedy and they were allowed to form more slowly. The Greek name for frankincense formed in this manner is "drop-incense" or "solid incense," and for the smaller kind "chick-pea incense"; the fragments knocked off by striking the tree we call manna. Even at the present day, however, drops are found that weigh as much as a third of a *mina*, that is 28 denarii. Alexander the Great in his boyhood was heaping frankincense on the altars in lavish fashion, when his tutor Leonides told him that he might worship the gods in that manner when he had conquered the frankincense-producing races; but when

Alexander had won Arabia he sent Leonides a ship with a cargo of frank-incense, with a message charging him to worship the gods without any stint.

Frankincense after being collected is conveyed to Sabota on camels, one of the gates of the city being opened for its admission; the kings have made it a capital offence for camels so laden to turn aside from the high road. At Sabota a tithe estimated by measure and not by weight is taken by the priests for the god they call Sabis, and the incense is not allowed to be put on the market until this has been done; this tithe is drawn on to defray what is a public expenditure, for actually on a fixed number of days the god graciously entertains guests at a banquet. It can only be exported through the country of the Gebbanitae, and accord-ingly a tax is paid on it to the king of that people as well. Their capital is Thomna, which is 1487½ miles distant from the town of Gaza in Judaea on the Mediterranean coast; the journey is divided into 65 stages with halts for camels. Fixed portions of the frankincense are also given to the priests and the king's secretaries, but beside these the guards and their attendants and the gate-keepers and servants also have their pickings: indeed all along the route they keep on paying, at one place for water, at another for fodder, or the charges for lodging at the halts, and the vari-ous octrois; so that expenses mount up to 688 denarii per camel before the Mediterranean coast is reached; and then again payment is made to the customs officers of our empire. Consequently the price of the best frankincense is 6, of the second best 5, and the third best 3 denarii a pound. It is tested by its whiteness and stickiness, its fragility and its readiness to catch fire from a hot coal; and also it should not give to pressure of the teeth, and should rather crumble into grains. Among us it is adulterated with drops of white resin, which closely resemble it, but the fraud can be detected by the means specified.

Some authorities have stated that myrrh is the product of a tree grow-ing in the same forests among the frankincense-trees, but the majority say that it grows separately; and in fact it occurs in many places in Ara-bia, as will appear when we deal with its varieties. A kind highly spoken of is also imported from islands, and the Sabaei[9] even cross the sea to the Cave-dwellers' Country to procure it. Also a cultivated variety is pro-duced which is much preferred to the wild kind. The plant enjoys being raked and having the soil round it loosened, as it is the better for having its roots cool.

[9]The Sabaeans lived in southern Arabia. The queen of Sheba who visited the biblical King Solomon was probably a Sabaean chief.

The tree grows to a height of nearly eight feet; it has thorns on it, and the trunk is hard and twisted, and thicker than that of the frankincense-tree, and even thicker at the root than in the remaining part of it. Authorities state that the bark is smooth and resembles that of the strawberry-tree, and others that it is rough and prickly; and they say that the leaf is that of the olive, but more wrinkled and with sharp points — though Juba says it is like that of the alexanders. Some say that it resembles the juniper, only that it is rougher and bristling with thorns, and that the leaf is rounder but tastes like juniper. Also there have been writers who have falsely asserted that the frankincense-tree produces myrrh as well as frankincense.

The myrrh-producing tree also is tapped twice a year at the same seasons as the frankincense-tree, but in its case the incisions are made all the way up from the root to those of the branches that are strong enough to bear it. But before it is tapped the tree exudes of its own accord a juice called stacte, which is the most highly valued of all myrrh. Next after this comes the cultivated kind, and also the better variety of the wild kind, the one tapped in summer. No tithes are given to a god from myrrh, as it also grows in other countries; however, the growers have to pay a quarter of the yield to the king of the Gebanitae. For the rest it is bought up all over the district from the common people and packed into leather bags; and our perfumiers have no difficulty in distinguishing the different sorts by the evidence of the scent and consistency. There are a great many varieties, the first among the wild kinds being the Cave-dweller myrrh, next the Minaean, which includes the Astramitic, Gebbanitic and Ausaritic from the kingdom of the Gebbanitae; the third quality is the Dianite, the fourth a mixture from various sources, the fifth the Sambracene from a seaboard state in the kingdom of the Sabaei, and the sixth the one called Dusirite. There is also a white kind found, in one place only, which is brought into the town of Mesalum for sale. The Cave-dweller kind is distinguished by its thickness and because it is rather dry and dusty and foreign in appearance, but has a stronger scent than the other sorts. The Sambracene variety is advertised as surpassing other kinds in its agreeable quality, but it has not a strong scent. Broadly speaking, however, the proof of goodness is given by its being in small pieces of irregular shape, forming in the solidifying of the juice as it turns white and dries up, and in its showing white marks like finger-nails when it is broken, and having a slightly bitter taste. The second best kind is mottled inside, and the worst is the one that is black inside; and if it is black outside as well it is of a still inferior quality.

The prices vary with the supply of buyers; that of stacte ranges from 3 to 50 denarii a pound, whereas the top price for cultivated myrrh is 11 denarii and for Erythrean 16 — this kind is passed off as Arabian — and for the kernel of Cave-dweller 16½, but for the variety called scented myrrh 12. Myrrh is adulterated with lumps of lentisk and with gum, and also with cucumber juice to give it a bitter taste, as it is with litharge of silver to increase its weight. The rest of the impurities can be detected by taste, and gum by its sticking to the teeth. But the adulteration most difficult to detect is that practised in the case of Indian myrrh, which is collected in India from a certain thorn-bush; this is the only commodity imported from India that is of worse quality than that of other countries — indeed it is easily distinguished because it is so very inferior. . . .

[The Source of Purple Dye]

And nevertheless [the pearl] is an almost everlasting piece of property — it passes to its owner's heir, it is offered for public sale like some landed estate; whereas every hour of use wears away robes of scarlet and purple, which the same mother, luxury, has made almost as costly as pearls.

Purples live seven years at most. They stay in hiding like the murex for 30 days at the time of the rising of the dog-star. They collect into shoals in spring-time, and their rubbing together causes them to discharge a sort of waxy viscous slime. The murex also does this in a similar manner, but it has the famous flower of purple, sought after for dyeing robes, in the middle of its throat: here there is a white vein of very scanty fluid from which that precious dye, suffused with a dark rose colour, is drained, but the rest of the body produces nothing. People strive to catch this fish alive, because it discharges this juice with its life; and from the larger purples they get the juice by stripping off the shell, but they crush the smaller ones alive with the shell, as that is the only way to make them disgorge the juice. The best Asiatic purple is at Tyre, the best African is at Meninx and on the Gaetulian coast of the Ocean, the best European in the district of Sparta. The official rods and axes of Rome clear it a path, and it also marks the honourable estate of boyhood; it distinguishes the senate from the knighthood, it is called in to secure the favour of the gods; and it adds radiance to every garment, while in a triumphal robe it is blended with gold. Consequently even the mad lust for the purple may be excused; but what is the cause of the prices paid for purple-shells, which have an unhealthy odour when used for dye and a gloomy tinge in their radiance resembling an angry sea?

The purple's tongue is an inch long; when feeding it uses it for piercing a hole in the other kinds of shell-fish, so hard is its point. These fish die in fresh water and wherever a river discharges into the sea, but otherwise when caught they live as much as seven weeks on their own slime. All shell-fish grow with extreme rapidity, especially the purplefish; they reach their full size in a year.

But if having come to this point our exposition were to pass over elsewhere, luxury would undoubtedly believe itself defrauded and would find us guilty of remissness. For this reason we will pursue the subject of manufactures as well, so that just as the principle of foodstuffs is learnt in food, so everybody who takes pleasure in the class of things in question may be well-informed on the subject of that which is the prize of their mode of life. Shell-fish supplying purple dyes and scarlets — the material of these is the same but it is differently blended — are of two kinds: the whelk is a smaller shell resembling the one that gives out the sound of a trumpet, whence the reason of its name, by means of the round mouth incised in its edge; the other is called the purple, with a channelled beak jutting out and the side of the channel tube-shaped inwards, through which the tongue can shoot out; moreover it is prickly all round, with about seven spikes forming a ring, which are not found in the whelk, though both shells have as many rings as they are years old. The trumpet-shell clings only to rocks and can be gathered round crags.

Another name used for the purple is "pelagia." There are several kinds, distinguished by their food and the ground they live on. The mud-purple feeds on rotting slime and the seaweed-purple on seaweed, both being of a very common quality. A better kind is the reef-purple, collected on the reefs of the sea, though this also is lighter and softer as well. The pebble-purple is named after a pebble in the sea, and is remarkably suitable for purple dyes; and far the best for these is the melting-purple, that is, one fed on a varying kind of mud. Purples are taken in a sort of little lobster-pot of fine ply thrown into deep water. These contain bait, cockles that close with a snap, as we observe that mussels do. These when half-killed but put back into the sea gape greedily as they revive and attract the purples, which go for them with outstretched tongues. But the cockles when pricked by their spike shut up and nip the creatures nibbling them. So the purples hang suspended because of their greed and are lifted out of the water.

It is most profitable for them to be taken after the rising of the dog-star or before spring-time, since when they have waxed themselves over with slime, they have their juices fluid. But this fact is not known to the dyers' factories, although it is of primary importance. Subsequently the vein of which we spoke is removed, and to this salt has to be added, about a pint for every hundred pounds; three days is the proper time for it to be steeped (as the fresher the salt the stronger it is), and it should be heated in a leaden pot, and with 50 lbs. of dye to every six gallons of water kept at a uniform and moderate temperature by a pipe brought from a furnace some way off. This will cause it gradually to deposit the portions of flesh which are bound to have adhered to the veins, and after about nine days the cauldron is strained and a fleece that has been washed clean is dipped for a trial, and the liquid is heated up until fair confidence is achieved. A ruddy colour is inferior to a blackish one. The fleece is allowed to soak for five hours and after it has been carded is dipped again, until it soaks up all the juice. The whelk by itself is not approved of, as it does not make a fast dye; it is blended in a moderate degree with sea-purple and it gives to its excessively dark hue that hard and brilliant scarlet which is in demand; when their forces are thus mingled, the one is enlivened, or deadened as the case may be, by the other. The total amount of dye-stuffs required for 1,000 lbs. of fleece is 200 lbs. of whelk and 111 lbs. of sea-purple; so is produced that remarkable amethyst colour. For Tyrian purple the wool is first soaked with sea-purple for a preliminary pale dressing, and then completely transformed with whelk dye. Its highest glory consists in the colour of congealed blood, blackish at first glance but gleaming when held up to the light; this is the origin of Homer's[10] phrase, "blood of purple hue."

I notice that the use of purple at Rome dates from the earliest times, but that Romulus[11] used it only for a cloak; as it is fairly certain that the first of the kings to use the bordered robe and broader purple stripe was Tullus Hostilius, after the conquest of the Etruscans. Cornelius Nepos, who died in the principate of the late lamented Augustus, says: "In my young days the violet purple dye was the vogue, a pound of which sold at 100 denarii; and not much later the red purple of Taranto. This was followed by the double-dyed Tyrian purple, which it was impossible to buy for 1000 denarii per pound. This was first used in a bordered robe by Publius Lentulus Spinther, curule aedile, but met with disapproval, though who does not use this purple for covering dining-couches now-a-days?" Spinther was aedile in the consulship of Cicero, 63 B.C. Stuff dipped twice over used at that time to be termed "double-dyed," and

---

[10] Homer, the Greek epic poet (ca. 850 BCE), is the author of the *Iliad* and the *Odyssey*.

[11] Romulus, one of the legendary founders of Rome, and his twin brother, Remus, were supposed to have been raised by a wolf.

was regarded as a lavish extravagance, but now almost all the more agreeable purple stuffs are dyed in this way.

In a purple-dyed dress the rest of the process is the same except that trumpet-shell dye is not used, and in addition the juice is diluted with water and with human urine in equal quantities; and only half the amount of dye is used. This produces that much admired paleness, avoiding deep colouration, and the more diluted the more the fleeces are stinted.

The prices for dyestuff vary in cheapness with the productivity of the coasts, but those who buy them at an enormous price should know that deep-sea purple nowhere exceeds 50 sesterces and trumpet-shell 100 sesterces per 100 lbs. But every end leads to fresh starts, and men make a sport of spending, and like doubling their sports by combining them and re-adulterating nature's adulterations, for instance staining tortoiseshells, alloying gold with silver to produce amber-metal ware, and adding copper to these to make Corinthian ware. It is not enough to have stolen for a dye the name of a gem, "sober-stone," but when finished it is made drunk again with Tyrian dye, so as to produce from the combination an outlandish name and a twofold luxury at one time; and when they have made shell-dye, they think it an improvement for it to pass into Tyrian. Repentance must have discovered this first, the artificer altering a product that he disapproved of; but reason sprang up next, and a defect was turned into a success by marvellous inventions, and a double path pointed out for luxury, so that one colour might be concealed by another, being pronounced to be made sweeter and softer by this process; and also a method to blend minerals, and dye with Tyrian a fabric already dyed with scarlet, to produce *hysgine* colour. The kermes, a red kernel of Galatia, as we shall say when dealing with the products of the earth, or else in the neighbourhood of Merida in Lusitania, is most approved. But, to finish off these famous dyes at once, the kernel when a year old has a viscous juice, and also after it is four years old the juice tends to disappear, so that it lacks strength both when fresh and when getting old.

We have amply dealt with the method whereby the beauty of men and women alike believes that it is rendered most abundant. . . .

[The Lighthouse at Alexandria]

Another towering structure built by a king is also extolled, namely the one that stands on Pharos, the island that commands the harbour at Alexandria. The tower is said to have cost 800 talents. We should not fail to mention the generous spirit shown by King Ptolemy,[12] whereby he allowed the name of the architect, Sostratus of Cnidos, to be inscribed on the very fabric of the building. It serves, in connection with the movements of ships at night, to show a beacon so as to give warning of shoals and indicate the entrance to the harbour. Similar beacons now burn brightly in several places, for instance at Ostia and Ravenna. The danger lies in the uninterrupted burning of the beacon, in case it should be mistaken for a star, the appearance of the fire from a distance being similar. The same architect is said to have been the very first to build a promenade supported on piers: this he did at Cnidos. . . .

[Gemstones]

The first Roman to own a collection of gemstones (for which we normally use the foreign term "dactyliotheca," or "ring cabinet") was Sulla's[13] stepson Scaurus. For many years there was no other until Pompey[14] the Great dedicated in the Capitol among his other offerings a ring cabinet that had belonged to King Mithridates.[15] This, as Varro and other authorities of the period confirm, was far inferior to that of Scaurus. Pompey's example was followed by Julius Caesar,[16] who during his dictatorship consecrated six cabinets of gems in the temple of Venus Genetrix, and by Marcellus, Octavia's son, who dedicated one in the temple of Apollo on the Palatine.

However, it was this victory of Pompey over Mithridates that made fashion veer to pearls and gemstones. The victories of Lucius Scipio and of Cnaeus Manlius had done the same for chased silver, garments of cloth of gold and dining couches inlaid with bronze; and that of Mummius for Corinthian bronzes and fine paintings. To make my point clearer, I shall append statements taken directly from official records of Pompey's triumphs. Thus, Pompey's third triumph was held on his own birthday, September 29th of the year in which Marcus Piso and Marcus Messala were consuls, to celebrate his conquest of the pirates, Asia, Pontus and all the peoples and kings mentioned in the seventh volume of this work. In this triumph, then, there was carried in the procession

[12] King Ptolemy II (ca. 308–246 BCE, r. 285–246 BCE).

[13] Sulla (138–78 BCE) was a Roman general and dictator (82–79 BCE).

[14] Pompey (106–48 BCE), a Roman general, was the rival of Julius Caesar.

[15] Mithridates, or Mithradates VI (ca. 120–63 BCE), king of Pontus, was defeated by Pompey in 66 BCE.

[16] Julius Caesar (100–44 BCE), a Roman general and statesman, became dictator in 45 BCE but was murdered a year later.

a gaming-board complete with a set of pieces, the board being made of two precious minerals and measuring three feet broad and four feet long. And in case anyone should doubt that our natural resources have become exhausted seeing that to-day no gems even approach such a size, there rested on this board a golden moon weighing 30 pounds. There were also displayed three gold dining couches; enough gold vessels inlaid with gems to fill nine display stands; three gold figures of Minerva,[17] Mars[18] and Apollo[19] respectively; thirty-three pearl crowns; a square mountain of gold with deer, lions and every variety of fruit on it and a golden vine entwined around it; and a grotto of pearls, on the top of which there was a sundial. Furthermore, there was Pompey's portrait rendered in pearls, that portrait so pleasing with the handsome growth of hair swept back from the forehead, the portrait of that noble head revered throughout the world—that portrait, I say, that portrait was rendered in pearls. Here it was austerity that was defeated and extravagance that more truly celebrated its triumph. Never, I think, would his surname "the Great" have survived among the stalwarts of that age had he celebrated his first triumph in this fashion! To think that it is of pearls, Great Pompey, those wasteful things meant only for women, of pearls, which you yourself cannot and must not wear, that your portrait is made! To think that this is how you make yourself seem valuable! Is not then the trophy that you placed upon the summit of the Pyrenees a better likeness of yourself? This, to be sure, would have been a gross and foul disgrace were it not rather to be deemed a cruel omen of Heaven's wrath. That head, so ominously manifested without its body in oriental splendour, bore a meaning which even then could not be mistaken.[20] But as for the rest of that triumph, how worthy it was of a good man and true! 200,000,000 sesterces were given to the State, 100,000,000 to the commanders and quaestors who had guarded the coasts and 6000 to each soldier. However, he merely made it easier for us to excuse the conduct of the Emperor Gaius when, apart from other effeminate articles of clothing, he wore slippers sewn with pearls, or that of the Emperor Nero, when he had scepters, actors' masks and travelling couches adorned with pearls. Why, we seem to have lost even the right to criticize cups and other pieces of household equipment inlaid with gems or, again, rings with stones set in open bezels. For compared

[17] Minerva was the goddess of wisdom and art in Roman mythology, equivalent to the Olympian goddess Athena.
[18] Mars was the god of war in Roman mythology.
[19] Apollo was the Olympian god of prophecy, music, poetry, medicine, and the sun.
[20] A reference to his murder in Egypt in 48 BCE. [Translator's note.]

with Pompey's, there is no extravagance that can be considered to have been so harmful.

It was the same victory that brought myrrhine ware for the first time to Rome. Pompey was the first to dedicate myrrhine bowls and cups, which he set aside from the spoils of his triumphs for Jupiter of the Capitol. Such vessels immediately passed into ordinary use, and there was a demand even for display stands and tableware. Lavish expenditure on this fashion is increasing every day. . . . an ex-consul, drank from a myrrhine cup for which he had given 70,000 sesterces, although it held just three pints. He was so fond of it that he would gnaw its rim; and yet the damage he thus caused only enhanced its value, and there is no other piece of myrrhine ware even to-day that has a higher price set upon it. The amount of money squandered by this same man upon the other articles of this material in his possession can be gauged from their number, which was so great that, when Nero took them away from the man's children and displayed them, they filled the private theatre in his gardens across the Tiber, a theatre which was large enough to satisfy even Nero's desire to sing before a full house at the time when he was rehearsing for his appearance in Pompey's theatre. It was at this time that I saw the pieces of a single broken cup included in the exhibition. It was decided that these, like the body of Alexander,[21] should be preserved in a kind of catafalque for display, presumably as a sign of the sorrows of the age and the ill-will of Fortune. When the ex-consul Titus Petronius was facing death, he broke, to spite Nero, a myrrhine dipper that had cost him 300,000 sesterces, thereby depriving the Emperor's dining-room table of this legacy. Nero, however, as was proper for an emperor, outdid everyone by paying 1,000,000 sesterces for a single bowl. That one who was acclaimed as a victorious general and as Father of his Country should have paid so much in order to drink is a detail that we must formally record.

Myrrhine vessels come to us from the East. There the substance is found in several otherwise unremarkable localities, particularly within the kingdom of Parthia. It is in Carmania, however, that the finest specimens exist. The substance is thought to be a liquid which is solidified underground by heat. In size the pieces are never larger than a small display stand, while in bulk they rarely equal the drinking vessels that we have discussed.

---

[21] Alexander the Great (356–323 BCE), king of Macedon, led conquest expeditions all the way to Central Asia and India, but died on the way back to Greece.

7

The Voyage around the Red Sea

First Century CE

*The Voyage around the Red Sea (in Greek, Periplus Maris Erythraei)
was a manual for Red Sea pilots who wanted to navigate along the coasts
of the Arabian Sea. Maris Erythraei means, literally, "Red Sea," but for
the Greeks that designation included the Persian Gulf and the Indian
Ocean. In the ports now located in Yemen and Oman, Greek-speaking
Roman traders obtained frankincense and myrrh from Arab traders for
the Mediterranean home market and to trade in India for goods from farther east. At ports around the mouth of the Indus River, they obtained silk
from China, spices from the Himalayas, and gems and tropical produce
from India and Southeast Asia. Some four hundred years after Alexander's conquest, Greek was still spoken in northwestern India, even in
areas never occupied by the Greeks. Take note of all the goods that were
part of the Silk Roads trade by the first century CE.*

The port of trade of Muza, though without a harbor, offers a good road-
stead for mooring because of the anchorages with sandy bottom all
around. Merchandise for which it offers a market are: purple cloth, fine
and ordinary quality; Arab sleeved clothing, either with no adornment
or with the common adornment or with checks or interwoven with gold
thread; saffron; *cyperus*;[1] cloth; *abollai*; blankets, in limited number,
with no adornment as well as with traditional local adornment; girdles
with shaded stripes; unguent, moderate amount; money, considerable
amount; wine and grain, limited quantity because the region produces
wheat in moderate quantity and wine in greater. To the king and the
governor are given [?]: horses and pack mules; goldware; embossed
silverware; expensive clothing; copperware. Its exports consist of local
products—myrrh, the select grade and *stacte*, the Abeirian [?] and

---

[1] *Cyperus* and other italicized words in this document name goods that cannot be
identified.

The Periplus Maris Erythraei, trans. and ed. Lionel Casson (Princeton, N.J.: Princeton
University Press, 1989), 63–67, 75–81.

Minaean; white marble—as well as all the aforementioned merchandise from Adulis across the water. The best time for sailing to this place is around the month of September, that is Thoth, though there is nothing to prevent leaving even earlier.

About a 300-stade[2] sail past this port, the Arabian mainland and the country of Barbaria across the water in the vicinity of Avalites converge to form a strait, not very long, that contracts the waters and closes them off into a narrow passage; here in the middle of the channel, 60 stades wide, stands Diodoros Island. For this reason, and because a wind blows down from the mountains that lie alongside, the sail through along the island meets strong currents. Along this strait is Okelis, an Arab village on the coast that belongs to the same province; it is not so much a port of trade as a harbor, watering station, and the first place to put in for those sailing on.

Beyond Okelis, with the waters again opening out towards the east and little by little being revealed to be open sea, about 1200 stades distant is Eudaimon Arabia, a village on the coast belonging to the same kingdom, Charibael's. It has suitable harbors and sources of water much sweeter than at Okelis. It stands at the beginning of a gulf formed by the receding of the shore. Eudaimon Arabia ["prosperous Arabia"], a full-fledged city in earlier days, was called Eudaimon when, since vessels from India did not go on to Egypt and those from Egypt did not dare sail to the places further on but came only this far, it used to receive the cargoes of both, just as Alexandria receives cargoes from overseas as well as from Egypt. And now, not long before our time, Caesar[3] sacked it.

Immediately after Eudaimon Arabia come a long coast and bay, populated by the villages of Nomads and Ichthyophagoi, that stretch for 2000 stades or more, at which point, beyond the projecting headland, is another port of trade on the coast, Kane, belonging to the kingdom of Eleazos, the frankincense-bearing land; near it are two barren islands, one called Orneon ["of the birds"] and the other Trullas, 120 stades offshore from Kane. Above it inland lies the metropolis of Saubatha, which is also the residence of the king. All the frankincense grown in the land is brought into Kane, as if to a warehouse, by camel as well as by rafts of a local type made of leathern bags, and by boats. It also carries on trade with the ports across the water—Barygaza, Skythia, Omana—and with its neighbor, Persis.

---

[2] A Greek measurement that equals 185 meters or 607 feet.
[3] Julius Caesar.

Its imports from Egypt are: wheat, limited quantity, and wine, just as to Muza; also as to Muza, Arab clothing, either with common adornment or no adornment or of printed fabric, in rather large quantities; copper; tin; coral; storax; and the rest of the items that go to Muza. Also, for the king, embossed silverware and money [?], rather large quantities, plus horses and statuary and fine-quality clothing with no adornment. It exports local wares, namely frankincense and aloe; the rest of its exports are through its connections with the other ports of trade. The time to set sail for this place is about the same as for Muza, but earlier.

After Kane, with the shoreline receding further, there next come another bay, very deep, called Sachalites, which extends for a considerable distance, and the frankincense-bearing land; this is mountainous, has a difficult terrain, an atmosphere close and misty, and trees that yield frankincense. The frankincense-bearing trees are neither very large nor tall; they give off frankincense in congealed form on the bark, just as some of the trees we have in Egypt exude gum. The frankincense is handled by royal slaves and convicts. For the districts are terribly unhealthy; harmful to those sailing by and absolutely fatal to those working there—who, moreover, die off easily because of the lack of nourishment. . . .

Vessels moor at Barbarikon, but all the cargoes are taken up the river to the king at the metropolis. In this port of trade there is a market for: clothing, with no adornment in good quantity, of printed fabric in limited quantity; multicolored textiles; peridot [?]; coral; storax; frankincense; glassware; silverware; money; wine, limited quantity. As return cargo it offers: costus; bdellium; *lykion*; nard; turquoise; lapis lazuli; Chinese pelts, cloth, and yarn; indigo.[4] Those who sail with the Indian [winds] leave around July, that is, Epeiph. The crossing with these is hard going but absolutely favorable and shorter.

After the Sinthos River there is another bay, hidden from view, to the north. It is named Eirinon, with the additional names Little and Big. Both are bodies of water with shoals and a succession of shallow eddies reaching a long way from land so that frequently, with the shore nowhere in sight, vessels will run aground and, if caught and thrust

---

[4] Not all these goods can be identified, but peridot is likely a kind of green stone, coral the red coral from the Mediterranean, storax a fragrance from tropical and semitropical regions, bdellium a fragrance from the dry region of West Asia, nard or spikenard a fragrance from a Himalayan herb, turquoise a semiprecious blue-green stone from Persia, and indigo a blue dye from India. Lapis lazuli was the most desired stone in the ancient world. Precious and blue in color, it was found only in Badakhshan in Central Asia.

further in, be destroyed. Beyond this bay a promontory juts out, curving from Eirinon first east and south and then west; it embraces the gulf called Barake, which itself embraces seven islands. Ships around its entrance that blunder in and then pull back the short distance into open water, escape; those that get closed inside the basin of Barake are destroyed. For not only are the waves there very big and oppressive, but the sea is choppy and turbid, with eddies and violent whirlpools. The bottom in some places has sheer drops, in others is rocky and sharp, so that the anchors lying parallel [i.e., dropped from the bows], thrust out to withstand [the difficult waters], get cut loose and some even get smashed on the sea floor. An indication of these [dangers] to vessels coming from the sea are the snakes, huge and black, that emerge to meet them. In the areas beyond, and around Barygaza, snakes that are smaller and yellow and golden in color are met with.

Immediately after the gulf of Barake is the gulf of Barygaza and the coast of the region of Ariake, the beginning both of Manbanos's realm and of all of India. The part inland, which borders on Skythia, is called Aberia, the part along the coast Syrastrene. The region, very fertile, produces grain, rice, sesame oil, ghee, cotton, and the Indian cloths made from it, those of ordinary quality. There are a great many herds of cattle, and the men are of very great size and dark skin color. The metropolis of the region is Minnagara, from which great quantities of cloth are brought to Barygaza. In the area there are still preserved to this very day signs of Alexander's[5] expedition, ancient shrines and the foundations of encampments and huge wells. The voyage along the coast of this region, from Barbarikon to the promontory near Astakapra across from Barygaza called Papike, is 3000 stades.

Beyond it is another gulf, on the inside of the waves, that forms an inlet directly to the north. Near the mouth is an island called Baiones, and, at the very head, a mighty river called the Mais. Vessels whose destination is Barygaza cross the gulf, which is about 300 stades wide, leaving the island, whose highest point is visible, to the left and heading due east toward the mouth of Barygaza's river. This river is called the Lamnaios.

This gulf which leads to Barygaza, since it is narrow, is hard for vessels coming from seaward to manage. For they arrive at either its right-hand side or its left-hand, and attempting it by the left-hand side is better than the other. For, on the right-hand side, at the very mouth of the gulf,

---

[5] Alexander the Great (356–323 BCE), king of Macedon, led conquest expeditions all the way to Central Asia and India, and died on the way back to Greece.

there extends a rough and rock-strewn reef called Herone, near the village of Kammoni. Opposite it, on the left-hand side, is the promontory in front of Astakapra called Papike; mooring here is difficult because of the current around it and because the bottom, being rough and rocky, cuts the anchor cables. And, even if you manage the gulf itself, the very mouth of the river on which Barygaza stands is hard to find because the land is low and nothing is clearly visible even from nearby. And, even if you find the mouth, it is hard to negotiate because of the shoals in the river around it.

For this reason local fishermen in the king's service come out with crews [of rowers] and long ships, the kind called *trappaga* and *kotymba*, to the entrance as far as Syrastrene to meet vessels and guide them up to Barygaza. Through the crew's efforts, they maneuver them right from the mouth of the gulf through the shoals and tow them to predetermined stopping places; they get them under way when the tide comes in and, when it goes out, bring them to anchor in certain harbors and basins. The basins are rather deep spots along the river up to Barygaza. For this lies on the river about 300 stades upstream from the mouth.

All over India there are large numbers of rivers with extreme ebb-and-flood tides that at the time of the new moon and the full moon last for up to three days, diminishing during the intervals. They are much more extreme in the area around Barygaza than elsewhere. Here suddenly the sea floor becomes visible, and certain parts along the coast, which a short while ago had ships sailing over them, at times become dry land, and the rivers, because of the inrush at flood tide of a whole concentrated mass of seawater, are driven headlong upstream against the natural direction of their flow for a good many stades.

Thus the navigating of ships in and out is dangerous for those who are inexperienced and are entering this port of trade for the first time. For, once the thrust of the flood tide is under way, restraining anchors do not stay in place. Consequently, the ships, carried along by its force and driven sideways by the swiftness of the current, run aground on the shoals, and break up, while smaller craft even capsize. Even in the channels some craft, if not propped up, will tilt over on their sides during the ebb and, when the flood suddenly returns, get swamped by the first wave of the flow. So much power is generated at the inrush of the sea even during the dark of the moon, particularly if the flood arrives at night, that when the tide is just beginning to come in and the sea is still at rest, there is carried from it to people at the mouth something like the rumble of an army heard from afar, and after a short while the sea itself races over the shoals with a hiss.

Inland behind Barygaza there are numerous peoples: the Aratriori, Arachusioi, Gandaraioi, and the peoples of Proklais, in whose area Bukephalos Alexandreia is located. And beyond these is a very warlike people, the Bactrians, under a king. . . . Alexander[6] setting out from these parts, penetrated as far as the Ganges but did not get to Limyrike and the south of India. Because of this, there are to be found on the market in Barygaza even today old drachmas engraved with the inscriptions, in Greek letters, of Apollodotus and Menander, rulers who came after Alexander.

There is in this region [of Barygaza] towards the east a city called Ozene, the former seat of the royal court, from which everything that contributes to the region's prosperity, including what contributes to trade with us, is brought down to Barygaza: onyx; agate [?]; Indian garments of cotton; garments of *molochinon*; and a considerable amount of cloth of ordinary quality. Through this region there is also brought down from the upper areas the nard that comes by way of Proklais (the Kattyburine, Patropapige, and Kabalite), the nard that comes through the adjacent part of Skythia, and costus and bdellium.

In this port of trade there is a market for: wine, principally Italian but also Laodicean and Arabian; copper, tin, and lead; coral and peridot [?]; all kinds of clothing with no adornment or of printed fabric; multi-colored girdles, eighteen inches wide; storax; yellow sweet clover [?]; raw glass; realgar; sulphide of antimony; Roman money, gold and silver, which commands an exchange at some profit against the local currency; unguent, inexpensive and in limited quantity. For the king there was imported in those times precious silverware, slave musicians, beautiful girls for concubinage, fine wine, expensive clothing with no adornment, and choice unguent. This area exports: nard; costus; bdellium; ivory; onyx; agate [?]; *lykion*; cotton cloth of all kinds; Chinese [silk] cloth; *molochinon* cloth; [silk] yarn; long pepper;[7] and items brought here from the [nearby] ports of trade. For those sailing to this port from Egypt, the right time to set out is around the month of July, that is Epeiph.

---

[6] This Alexander is a Greek king who ruled Bactria and made an incursion into India.
[7] Again, not all these goods can be identified. Onyx is a precious stone with bands of different color, and agate has similar features.

8

PTOLEMY

The Geography

Mid-Second Century CE

The Greek scholar Ptolemy (ca. 100–170 CE), who lived in Alexandria at the height of the Roman Empire's prestige and power, wrote about astronomy, mathematics, and geography. Because he was a Greek, most of his information about Central Asia came from Hellenistic sources, some of them probably dating back to the time of Alexander. Ptolemy invented the system of locating places in grids that later developed into the longitudes and latitudes of modern cartography. At this time, Bactria and Sogdiana were part of the Kushan Empire, yet Ptolemy used Greek place names for these regions and knew that the Greek language was still in use there. Look for the kinds of information Ptolemy provides.

Chapter XI

LOCATION OF BACTRIANA
(SEVENTH MAP OF ASIA)

On the west Bactriana is bounded by Margiana; on the north and also on the east by Sogdiana and a part of the Oxus river; on the south by the part of Aria which extends from the terminus in the confines of Margiana to the terminus in   111   30   39
and along the parallel of Paropanisadus an equal distance through the mountains to the sources of the Oxus which are located
in   119   30   39
    Rivers flow through Bactria which rivers empty into the Oxus, and the
Oxus river, the sources of which are in   110   39
the Dargamanis, the sources of which are in   116   30   36   40
the Zariaspes the sources of which are in   113   39

Ptolemy, *Ptolemy's Geography*, trans. and ed. E. L. Stevenson (New York: New York Public Library, 1932), 6:142–43.

the Artamis the sources of which are in	114		39
the Dargoedus the sources of which are in	116		39
it flows into the Oxus in	116	30	44

the others are the Artamis and the Zariaspes which, after uniting their waters in 113 40

they flow into the Oxus in 112 30 44

the Dargamanis moreover after uniting with the rivers in the

location	109	40	10
flows into the Oxus	109	44	20

The *Salaterae* and the *Zariaspae* inhabit northern Bactria along the Oxus river; toward the south below the *Salaterae* are the *Chomari*; below whom are the *Comi*, then the *Acinacae*, then the *Tambyzi*; below Zariaspa are the *Tochari* a great race;[1] below these are the *Marycaei*, the *Scordac* and the *Varni*, and below these are the *Sabadi*; and next below *Sabadi* are the *Orsipi* and the *Amarispi*.

The Bactrian towns in that part near the Oxus are

Charracharta	110		44	10
Zarispa	115		44	
Choana	117		42	
Suragana	117	30	40	30
Phratrua	119		39	20
near the other rivers				
Alicodra	107	30	43	30
Chomara	106	30	42	30
Curiandra	109	30	12	10
Cavaris	111	20	43	
Astacana	112		43	20
Evusmi regia	108	20	41	10
Menapia	113		41	20
Eucratidia	115		42	
Bactra regia	116		41	
Estobara	109	30	39	40
Maracanda	112		39	15
Maracodra	115	40	39	40

[1] A nomadic tribe arrived from Central Asian steppe, probably in the Yuezhi confederation.

Chapter XII

LOCATION OF SOGDIANA
(SEVENTH MAP OF ASIA)

The boundary of Sogdiana on the west is a part of Scythia near the section of the Oxus river which runs along the confines of Bactria and Margiana, then through the Oxius mountains near the Jaxartes river in   110   49
on the north by a part of Scythia along the Jaxartes river where it bends near the terminus which is in   120   48   30
on the east alone by the Sacara region along the Jaxartes river where it bends from the sources in   125   43
and along a direct line to the terminus which is located in   125   38   30
on the south and the west by Bactriana along the Oxus, which section we have noted, and near the Causasus mountains which are called the mountains of India, to the line which connects the indicated terminus and the sources of the Oxus river   119   30   39
     The mountains between the rivers of Sogdiana have their termini in   111   47
and   122   46   30
one of its rivers flows from the Oxia lake, the middle of which is located in   111   45
and there are other rivers flowing from these mountains called the Comedarum from which the Jaxartes flows, and into which river they empty; another is called the Dymus, the sources of which are in   124   43
where it joins with the Jaxartes   123   47
another of these rivers is called the Bascatis, the sources of which are in   123   43
and where it unites with the Jaxartes   121   47   30
     In parts of the region near the Oxius mountains the *Pasicae* dwell, near the section of Jaxartes on the north dwell the *Iali* and the *Tachori*, below whom are the *Augali*; then next to the Sogdios mountains are the *Oxydrancae*, the *Drybactae* and the *Candari*, and below the mountains are the *Mardyeni*; and near the Oxius are the *Oxiani* and the *Chorasmi*; in the parts which are near these toward the east dwell the *Drepsiani* bordering both of the rivers; and near these but more toward the source are the *Aristenses* near the Jaxartes, the *Cirrodaces* near the Oxus; and between the Caucasus mountains and Imaus mountains the region is called Vandabanda.

The mountain towns of Sogdiana near the banks of the Jaxartes are

Cyrescha	125		46	20
and near the Oxus				
Oxiana	117	30	44	40
Maruca	117	15	43	40
Cholbisina	117	40	41	
between the rivers and more remote				
Trybactra	112	15	45	30
Alexandria Oxiana	113		44	40
Indicomordana	115		44	40
Drepsa metropolis	120		45	
Alexandria ultima	122		41	

3

The Kushan Empire and the Influence of Buddhism, Second Century BCE–Second Century CE

9

The Questions of King Milinda

ca. 166–150 BCE

King Milinda, known to the Greeks as Menander, was an Indo-Greek king who ruled northwestern India before the coming of the Kushans. He was interested in the theology and practices of Buddhism but was puzzled by seeming contradictions. Thus he invited a Buddhist scholar, Nāgasena, to discuss them with him. The Buddhist sage agreed to the discussion, with the condition that they meet as scholars, not as king and subject. Presumably, the discussion was recorded, and it became a Buddhist text, The Questions of King Milinda. *How did the Greek king's curiosity about Buddhist theology reflect changes in Buddhism itself? To what extent were these changes caused by the cosmopolitan culture of the Silk Roads?*

On Honours Paid to the Buddha

Then Milinda the king, having thus been granted leave, fell at the feet of the teacher, and raising his clasped hands to his forehead, said: "Venerable Nāgasena, these leaders of other sects say thus: 'If the Buddha accepts gifts he cannot have passed entirely away. He must be still in union with the world, a shareholder in the things of the world; and therefore any honour paid to him becomes empty and vain. On the other

The Questions of King Milinda, trans. Rhys David (Oxford, U.K.: Oxford University Press, 1890), in *Sacred Books of the East,* 35:144–53, 246–48.

84

hand if he be entirely passed away [from life], unattached to the world, escaped from all existence, then honours would not be offered to him. For he who is entirely set free accepts no honour, and any act done to him who accepts it not becomes empty and vain.' This is a dilemma which has two horns. It is not a matter within the scope of those who have no mind it is a question fit for the great. Tear asunder this net of heresy, put it on one side. To you has this puzzle been put. Give to the future sons of the Conqueror eyes wherewith to see the riddle to the confusion of their adversaries."

"The Blessed One, O king," replied the Elder, "is entirely set free. And the Blessed One accepts no gift. Even at the foot of the Tree of Wisdom he abandoned all accepting of gifts, how much more then [sic] now when he has passed entirely away by that kind of passing away which leaves no root over [for the formation of a new existence]. For this, O king, has been said by Sariputta, the commander of the faith:

'Though worshipped, these Unequalled Ones, alike
By gods and men, unlike them all they heed
Neither a gift nor worship. They accept
It not, neither refuse it. Through the ages
All Buddhas were so, so will ever be!'

The king said: "Venerable Nāgasena, a father may speak in praise of his son, or a son of his father. But that is no ground for putting the adversaries to shame. It is only an expression of their own belief. Come now! Explain this matter to me fully to the establishing of your own doctrine, and to the unravelling of the net of the heretics."

The Elder replied: "The Blessed One, O king, is entirely set free [from life]. And the Blessed One accepts no gift. If gods or men put up a building to contain the jewel treasure of the relics of a Tathagata who does not accept their gift, still by that homage paid to the attainment of the supreme good under the form of the jewel treasure of his wisdom do they themselves attain to one or other of the three glorious states.[1] Suppose, O king, that though a great and glorious fire had been kindled, it should die out, would it then again accept any supply of dried grass or sticks?"

---

[1] That is, to another life as a man, or as a god, or to Arahatship here, on earth, in this birth. [Translator's note.]

"Even as it burned, Sir, it could not be said to accept fuel, how much less when it had died away, and ceased to burn, could it, an unconscious thing, accept it?"

"And when that one mighty fire had ceased, and gone out, would the world be bereft of fire?"

"Certainly not. Dry wood is the seat, the basis of fire, and any men who want fire can, by the exertion of their own strength and power, such as resides in individual men, once more, by twirling the fire-stick, produce fire, and with that fire do any work for which fire is required."

"Then that saying of the sectarians that 'an act done to him who accepts it not is empty and vain' turns out to be false. As that great and glorious fire was set alight, even so, great king, was the Blessed One set alight in the glory of his Buddhahood over the ten thousand world systems. As it went out, so has he passed away into that kind of passing away in which no root remains. As the fire, when gone out, accepted no supply of fuel, just so, and for the good of the world, has his accepting of gifts ceased and determined. As men, when the fire is out, and has no further means of burning, then by their own strength and effort, such as resides in individual men, twirl the fire-stick and produce fire, and do any work for which fire is required—so do gods and men, though a Tathagata has passed away and no longer accepts their gifts, yet put up a house for the jewel treasure of his relics, and doing homage to the attainment of supreme good under the form of the jewel treasure of his wisdom, they attain to one or other of the three glorious states. Therefore is it, great king, that acts done to the Tathagata, notwithstanding his having passed away and not accepting them, are nevertheless of value and bear fruit.

"Now hear, too, another reason for the same thing. Suppose, O king, there were to arise a great and mighty wind, and that then it were to die away. Would that wind acquiesce in being produced again?

"A wind that has died away can have no thought or idea of being reproduced. And why? Because the element wind is an unconscious thing.

"Or even, O king, would the word 'wind' be still applicable to that wind, when it had so died away?"

"Certainly not, Sir. But fans and punkahs are means for the production of wind. Any men who are oppressed by heat, or tormented by fever, can by means of fans and punkahs, and by the exertion of their own strength and power, such as resides in individual men, produce a breeze, and by that wind allay their heat, or assuage their fever."

"Then that saying of the sectarians that 'an act done to him who accepts it not is empty and vain' turns out to be false. As the great and mighty wind which blew, even so, great king, has the Blessed One blown over the ten thousand world systems with the wind of his love, so cool, so sweet, so calm, so delicate. As it first blew, and then died away, so has the Blessed One, who once blew with the wind so cool, so sweet, so calm, so delicate, of his love, now passed away with that kind of passing away in which no root remains. As those men were oppressed by heat and tormented with fever, even so are gods and men tormented and oppressed with threefold fire and heat.[2] As fans and punkahs are means of producing wind, so the relics and the jewel treasure of the wisdom of a Tathagata are means of producing the threefold attainment. And as men oppressed by heat and tormented by fever can by fans and punkahs produce a breeze, and thus allay the heat and assuage the fever, so can gods and men by offering reverence to the relics, and the jewel treasure of the wisdom of a Tatha-gata, though he has died away and accepts it not, cause goodness to arise within them, and by that goodness can assuage and can allay the fever and the torment of the threefold fire. Therefore is it, great king, that acts done to the Tathagata, notwithstanding his having passed away and not accepting them, are nevertheless of value and bear fruit.

"Now hear another reason for the same thing. Suppose, O king, a man were to make a drum sound, and then that sound were to die away. Would that sound acquiesce in being produced again?"

"Certainly not, Sir. The sound has vanished. It can have no thought or idea of being reproduced. The sound of a drum when it has once been produced and died away, is altogether cut off. But, Sir, a drum is a means of producing sound. And any man, as need arises, can by the effort of power residing in himself, beat on that drum, and so produce a sound."

"Just so, great king, has the Blessed One—except the teacher and the instruction he has left in his doctrine and discipline, and the jewel treasure of his relics whose value is derived from his righteousness, and contemplation, and wisdom, and emancipation, and insight given by the knowledge of emancipation—just so has he passed away by that kind of passing away in which no root remains. But the possibility of receiving the three attainments is not cut off because the Blessed One has passed away. Beings oppressed by the sorrow of becoming can, when they desire the attainments, still receive them by means of the jewel treasure of his relics and of his doctrine and discipline and teaching. Therefore is it, great king, that all acts done to the Tathagata, notwithstanding his having passed away and not accepting, are nevertheless of value and bear fruit. And this future possibility, great king, has been foreseen by

[2] That is, the three fires of lust, ill-will, and delusion, the going out of which is the state called, par excellence, "the going out" (Nirvana). [Translator's note.]

the Blessed One, and spoken of, and declared, and made known, when he said: 'It may be, Ananda, that in some of you the thought may arise: "The word of the Master is ended. We have no Teacher more!" But it is not thus, Ananda, that you should regard it. The Truth which I have preached to you, the Rules which I have laid down for the Order, let them, when I am gone, be the Teacher to you.' So that because the Tathagata has passed away and consents not thereto, that therefore any act done to him is empty and vain—this saying of the enemy is proved false. It is untrue, unjust, not according to fact, wrong, and perverse. It is the cause of sorrow, has sorrow as its fruit, and leads down the road to perdition!

"Now hear another reason for the same thing. Does the broad earth acquiesce, O king, in all kinds of seeds being planted all over it?"

"Certainly not, Sir."

"Then how is it those seeds, planted without the earth's consent, do yet stand fast and firmly rooted, and expand into trees with great trunks and sap and branches, and bearing fruits and flowers?"

"Though the earth, Sir, gives no consent, yet it acts as a site for those seeds, as a means of their development. Planted on that site they grow, by its means, into such great trees with branches, flowers, and fruit."

"Then, great king, the sectaries are destroyed, defeated, proved wrong by their own words when they say that 'an act done to him who accepts it not is empty and vain.' As the broad earth, O king, is the Tathagata, the Arahat, the Buddha supreme. Like it he accepts nothing. Like the seeds which through it attain to such developments are the gods and men who, through the jewel treasures of the relics and the wisdom of the Tathagata—though he have passed away and consent not to it—being firmly rooted by the roots of merit, become like unto trees casting a goodly shade by means of the trunk of contemplation, the sap of true doctrine, and the branches of righteousness, and bearing the flowers of emancipation, and the fruits of Samanaship. Therefore is it, great king, that acts done to the Tathagata, notwithstanding his having passed away and not accepting them, are still of value and bear fruit.

"Now hear another and further reason for the same thing. Do camels, buffaloes, asses, goats, oxen, or men acquiesce in the birth of worms inside them?"

"Certainly not, Sir."

"Then how is it then, that without their consent worms are so born, and spread by rapid reproduction of sons and grandsons?"

"By the power of evil Karma, Sir."

"Just so, great king, is it by the power of the relics and the wisdom of the Tathagata, who has passed away and acquiesces in nothing, that an act done to him is of value and bears fruit.

"Now hear another and further reason for the same thing. Do men consent, O king, that the ninety-eight diseases should be produced in their bodies?"

"Certainly not, Sir."

"Then how is it the diseases come?"

"By evil deeds done in former births."

"But, great king, if evil deeds done in a former birth have to be suffered here and now, then both good and evil done here or done before has weight and bears fruit. Therefore is it that acts done to the Tathagata, notwithstanding his having passed away and not consenting, are nevertheless of value and bear fruit.

"Now hear another and further reason for the same thing. Did you ever hear, O king, of the ogre named Nandaka, who, having laid hands upon the Elder Sariputta, was swallowed up by the earth?"

"Yes, Sir, that is matter of common talk among men."

"Well, did Sariputta acquiesce in that?"

"Though the world of gods and men, Sir, were to be destroyed, though the sun and moon were to fall upon the earth, though Sineru the king of mountains were to be dissolved, yet would not Sariputta the Elder have consented to any pain being inflicted on a fellow creature. And why not? Because every condition of heart which could cause him to be angry or offended has been in him destroyed and rooted out. And as all cause thereof had thus been removed, Sir, therefore could not Sariputta be angered even with those who sought to deprive him of his life."

"But if Sariputta, O king, did not consent to it, how was it that Nandaka was so swallowed up?"

"By the power of his evil deeds."

"Then if so, great king, an act done to him who consents not is still of power and bears fruit. And if this is so of an evil deed, how much more of a good one? Therefore is it, O king, that acts done to the Tathagata, notwithstanding his having passed away and not accepting them, are nevertheless of value and bear fruit.

"Now how many, O king, are those men who, in this life, have been swallowed up by the earth? Have you heard anything on that point?"

"Yes, Sir, I have heard how many there are."

"Then tell me."

"Kinka the Brahmin woman, and Suppabuddha the Sakyan, and Devadatta the Elder, and Nandaka the ogre, and Nanda the Brahman—these are the five people who were swallowed up by the earth."

"And whom, O king, had they wronged?"

"The Blessed One and his disciples."

"Then did the Blessed One or his disciples consent to their being so swallowed up?"

"Certainly not, Sir."

"Therefore is it, O king, that an act done to the Tathagata, notwithstanding his having passed away and not consenting thereto, is nevertheless of value and bears fruit." . . .

Adoration of Relics

"Venerable Nāgasena, the Tathagata said: 'Hinder not yourselves, Ananda, by honouring the remains of the Tathagata.' And on the other hand he said:

> 'Honour that relic of him who is worthy of honour,
> Acting in that way you go from this world to heaven.'

"Now if the first injunction was right the second must be wrong, and if the second is right the first must be wrong. This too is a double-edged problem now put to you, and you have to solve it."

"Both the passages you quote were spoken by the Blessed One. But it was not to all men, it was to the sons of the Conqueror that it was said: 'Hinder not yourselves, Ananda, by honouring the remains of the Tathagata.' Paying reverence is not the work of the sons of the Conqueror, but rather the grasping of the true nature of all compounded things, the practice of thought, contemplation in accordance with the rules of Satipatthana, the seizing of the real essence of all objects of thought, the struggle against evil, and devotion to their own [spiritual] good. These are things which the sons of the Conqueror ought to do, leaving to others, whether gods or men, the paying of reverence.

"And that is so, O king, just as it is the business of the princes of the earth to learn all about elephants, and horses, and chariots, and bows, and rapiers, and documents, and the law of property, to carry on the traditions of the Khattiya[3] clans, and to fight themselves and to lead others in war, while husbandry, merchandise, and the care of cattle are the business of other folk, ordinary Vessas and Suddas. — Or just as the business of Brahmins and their sons is concerned with the Rig-veda, the Yagur-veda, the Sama-veda, the Atharva-veda, with the knowledge

---

[3] *Khattiya* is a corrupt form of *Ksatriya* (in Sanskrit), the second caste in the Brahmanical system. Buddha spoke a vernacular language instead of the orthodox Sanskrit, and *The Questions of King Milinda* was composed in a northern Indian vernacular.

of lucky marks [on the body], of legends, Puranas,[4] lexicography, prosody, phonology, verses, grammar, etymology, astrology, interpretation of omens, and of dreams, and of signs, study of the six Vedangas, of eclipses of the sun and moon, of the prognostications to be drawn from the flight of comets, the thunderings of the gods, the junctions of planets, the fall of meteors, earthquakes, conflagrations, and signs in the heavens and on the earth, the study of arithmetic, of casuistry, of the interpretation of the omens to be drawn from dogs, and deer, and rats, and mixtures of liquids, and the sounds and cries of birds—while husbandry, merchandise, and the care of cattle are the business of other folk, ordinary Vessas and Suddas. So it was, O king, in the sense of 'Devote not yourselves to such things as are not your business, but to such things as are so' that the Tathagata was speaking when he said: 'Hinder not yourselves, Ananda, by honouring the remains of the Tathagata.' And if, O king, he had not said so, then would the Bhikkhus have taken his bowl and his robe, and occupied themselves with paying reverence to the Buddha through them!"

"Very good, Nāgasena! That is so, and I accept it as you say."

[4] Puranas are, literally, things in the past. They are among the numerous sacred texts of the Hindus.

10

The Lotus of the True Law
First Century BCE–First Century CE

The Lotus of the True Law *is a Buddhist text that reveals how Mahayana Buddhism encouraged and promoted Silk Roads trade. It was one of the earliest Buddhist texts composed in Sanskrit, rather than Pali and other vernacular languages used in early Buddhism, and among the first Buddhist texts to be translated into Chinese. During Kushan times, Mahayana became the dominant school in Buddhism. Mahayana*

The Saddharma-Pundarika; or, The Lotus of the True Law, trans. H. Kern, in *The Sacred Books of the East*, Book XXIV (Oxford, U.K.: Oxford University Press, 1884), 21:406–9.

Buddhists worshipped many bodhisattvas, and Avalokitesvara was one of the most powerful. According to The Lotus of the True Law, *he did not provide a paradise in which devotees could rest before proceeding to nirvana but saved people who were in trouble. Therefore traders and pilgrims made donations to him in the shrines that housed his image. From what dangers did the traders and pilgrims seek protection? Why do you think Avalokitesvara was the most popular deity among travelers on the Silk Roads?*

Thereafter the Bodhisattva Mahasattva Akshayamati rose from his seat, put his upper robe upon one shoulder, stretched his joined hands towards the Lord, and said: For what reason, O Lord, is the Bodhisattva Mahasattva Avalokitesvara called Avalokitesvara? So he asked, and the Lord answered to the Bodhisattva Mahasattva Akshayamati: All the hundred thousands of myriads of kotis[1] of creatures, young man of good family, who in this world are suffering troubles will, if they hear the name of the Bodhisattva Mahasattva Avalokitesvara, be released from that mass of troubles. Those who shall keep the name of this Bodhisattva Mahasattva Avalokitesvara, young man of good family, will, if they fall into a great mass of fire, be delivered therefrom by virtue of the lustre of the Bodhisattva Mahasattva. In case, young man of good family, creatures, carried off by the current of rivers, should implore the Bodhisattva Mahasattva Avalokitesvara, all rivers will afford them a ford. In case, young man of good family, many hundred thousand myriads of kotis of creatures, sailing in a ship on the ocean, should see their bullion, gold, gems, pearls, lapis lazuli, conch shells, stones [?], corals, emeralds, Musaragalvas, red pearls [?], and other goods lost, and the ship by a vehement, untimely gale cast on the island of Giantesses, and if in that ship a single being implores Avalokitesvara, all will be saved from that island of Giantesses. For that reason, young man of good family, the Bodhisattva Mahasattva Avalokitesvara is named Avalokitesvara.[2]

If a man given up to capital punishment implores Avalokitesvara, young man of good family, the swords of the executioners shall snap asunder. Further, young man of good family, if the whole triple chiliocosm were teeming with goblins and giants, they would by virtue of the

[1] Ten million, the highest unit in the numbering of that time.
[2] *Avalokita* means "beheld"; it is as such synonymous with *drishta*, seen, visible, and *pratyaksha*, visible, manifest, present. The bodhisattva is everywhere present, and therefore implored in need and danger. [Translator's note.]

name of the Bodhisattva Mahasattva Avalokitesvara being pronounced lose the faculty of sight in their wicked designs. If some creature, young man of good family, shall be bound in wooden or iron manacles, chains or fetters, be he guilty or innocent, then those manacles, chains or fetters shall give way as soon as the name of the Bodhisattva Mahasattva Avalokitesvara is pronounced. Such, young man of good family, is the power of the Bodhisattva Mahasattva Avalokitesvara. If this whole triple chiliocosm, young man of good family, were teeming with knaves, enemies, and robbers armed with swords, and if a merchant leader of a caravan marched with a caravan rich in jewels; if then they perceived those robbers, knaves, and enemies armed with swords, and in their anxiety and fright thought themselves helpless; if further, that leading merchant spoke to the caravan in this strain: Be not afraid, young gentlemen, be not frightened; invoke, all of you, with one voice the Bodhisattva Mahasattva Avalokitesvara, the giver of safety; then you shall be delivered from this danger by which you are threatened at the hands of robbers and enemies; if then the whole caravan with one voice invoked Avalokitesvara with the words: Adoration, adoration be to the giver of safety, to Avalokitesvara Bodhisattva Mahasattva! then, by the mere act of pronouncing that name, the caravan would be released from all danger. Such, young man of good family, is the power of the Bodhisattva Mahasattva Avalokitesvara. In case creatures act under the impulse of impure passion, young man of good family, they will, after adoring the Bodhisattva Mahasattva Avalokitesvara, be freed from passion. Those who act under the impulse of hatred will, after adoring the Bodhisattva Mahasattva Avalokitesvara, be freed from hatred. Those who act under the impulse of infatuation will, after adoring the Bodhisattva Mahasattva Avalokitesvara, be freed from infatuation. So mighty, young man of good family, is the Bodhisattva Mahasattva Avalokitesvara. If a woman, desirous of male offspring, young man of good family, adores the Bodhisattva Avalokitesvara, she shall get a son, nice, handsome, and beautiful; one possessed of the characteristics of a male child, generally beloved and winning, who has planted good roots. If a woman is desirous of getting a daughter, a nice, handsome, beautiful girl shall be born to her; one possessed of the (good) characteristics of a girl, generally beloved and winning, who has planted good roots. Such, young man of good family, is the power of the Bodhisattva Mahasattva Avalokitesvara.

11

The Amitabha Sutra

First Century BCE–First Century CE

Amitabha (also known as Amitayus) was an influential bodhisattva residing in the Western Pure Land, a paradise full of the Seven Treasures, among them the gems, silks, and other luxuries traded on the Silk Roads. He welcomed all willing to go there, even if they did not make the decision until they were on their deathbeds. Because the Western Pure Land was so beautiful and Bodhisattva Amitabha always on call to take people in, his followers were even more numerous than those of Avalokitesvara (Document 10). This text was also translated into Chinese, and the image of Amitabha later became the fat sitting Buddha who blesses devotees while attracting donations. As a sutra, this short text is meant to be learned by heart and recited continuously by devotees. Why was Amitabha transformed into the popular fat smiling Buddha?

Adoration to the Omniscient!

Thus it was heard by me: At one time the Blessed [Bhagavat, i.e. Buddha] dwelt at Sravasti,[1] in the Geta-grove, in the garden of Anathapindaka, together with a large company of Bhikshus [mendicant friars], viz. with twelve hundred and fifty Bhikshus, all of them acquainted with the five kinds of knowledge, elders, great disciples, and Arhats,[2] such as Sariputra, the elder, Mahamaudgalyayana, Mahakasyapa, Mahakapphina, Mahakatyayana, Mahakaushthila, Revata, Suddhipanthaka, Nanda, Ananda, Rahula, Gavampati, Bharadvaga, Kalodayin, Vakkula, and Aniruddha. He dwelt together with these and many other great disciples, and together with many noble-minded Bodhisattvas, such as Mangusrî, the prince, the Bodhisattva Agita, the Bodhisattva Gandhahastin, the Bodhisattva Nityodyukta, the Bodhisattva Anikshiptadhura. He dwelt together

---

[1] Sravasti, capital of the Northern Kosalas, residence of King Prasenagit. [Translator's note.]
[2] The great disciples of the Buddha.

The Smaller Sukhavati-vyuha, trans. J. Takakusu, *The Sacred Books of the East*, Book 49 (Oxford, U.K.: Oxford University Press, 1894), 49:89–102.

with them and many other noble-minded Bodhisattvas, and with Sakra, the Indra or King of the Devas,[3] and with Brahman Sahampati. With these and many other hundred thousand nayutas of sons of the gods, Bhagavat dwelt at Sravasti.

Then Bhagavat addressed the honoured Sariputra and said, "O Sariputra, after you have passed from here over a hundred thousand kotis of Buddha countries there is in the Western part a Buddha country, a world called Sukhavati [the happy country]. And there a Tathagata, called Amitayus, an Arhat, fully enlightened, dwells now and remains and supports himself, and teaches the Law.

"Now what do you think, Sariputra, for what reason is that world called Sukhavati [the happy]? In that world Sukhavati, O Sariputra, there is neither bodily nor mental pain for living beings. The sources of happiness are innumerable there. For that reason is that world called Sukhavati [the happy].

"And again, O Sariputra, that world Sukhavati is adorned with seven terraces, with seven rows of palm-trees, and with strings of bells. It is enclosed on every side, beautiful, brilliant with the four gems, viz. gold, silver, beryl, and crystal. With such arrays of excellences peculiar to a Buddha country is that Buddha country adorned.

"And again, O Sariputra, in that world Sukhavati there are lotus lakes, adorned with the seven gems, viz. gold, silver, beryl, crystal, red pearls, diamonds, and corals as the seventh. They are full of water which possesses the eight good qualities,[4] their waters rise as high as the fords and bathing-places, so that even crows may drink there; they are strewn with golden sand. And in these lotus-lakes there are all around on the four sides four stairs, beautiful and brilliant with the four gems, viz. gold, silver, beryl, crystal. And on every side of these lotus-lakes gem-trees are growing, beautiful and brilliant with the seven gems, viz. gold, silver, beryl, crystal, red pearls, diamonds, and corals as the seventh. And in those lotus-lakes lotus-flowers are growing, blue, blue-coloured, of blue splendour, blue to behold; yellow, yellow-coloured, of yellow splendour, yellow to behold; red, red-coloured, of red splendour, red to behold; white, white-coloured, of white splendour, white to behold; beautiful, beautifully-coloured, of beautiful splendour, beautiful to behold, and in circumference as large as the wheel of a chariot.

---

[3] Sakra is the Buddhist name for Indra, the king of Devas, or gods.
[4] The eight good qualities of water are limpidity and purity, refreshing coolness, sweetness, softness, fertilizing qualities, calmness, power of preventing famine, productiveness. [Translator's note.]

"And again, O Sariputra, in that Buddha country there are heavenly musical instruments always played on, and the earth is lovely and of golden colour. And in that Buddha country a flower-rain of heavenly Mandarava blossoms pours down three times every day, and three times every night. And the beings who are born there worship before their morning meal a hundred thousand koṭis of Buddhas by going to other worlds; and having showered a hundred thousand koṭis of flowers upon each Tathagata, they return to their own world in time for the afternoon rest. With such arrays of excellences peculiar to a Buddha country is that Buddha country adorned.

"And again, O Sariputra, there are in that Buddha country swans, curlews, and peacocks. Three times every night, and three times every day, they come together and perform a concert, each uttering his own note. And from them thus uttering proceeds a sound proclaiming the five virtues, the five powers, and the seven steps leading towards the highest knowledge. When the men there hear that sound, remembrance of Buddha, remembrance of the Law, remembrance of the Church, rises in their mind.

"Now, do you think, O Sariputra, that there are beings who have entered into the nature of animals [birds, &c]? This is not to be thought of. The very name of hells is unknown in that Buddha country, and likewise that of [descent into] animal bodies and of the realm of Yama [the four apayas].[5] No, these tribes of birds have been made on purpose by the Tathagata Amitayus, and they utter the sound of the Law. With such arrays of excellences, &c.

"And again, O Sariputra, when those rows of palm-trees and strings of bells in that Buddha country are moved by the wind, a sweet and enrapturing sound proceeds from them. Yes, O Sariputra, as from a heavenly musical instrument consisting of a hundred thousand koṭis of sounds, when played by Aryas, a sweet and enrapturing sound proceeds, a sweet and enrapturing sound proceeds from those rows of palm-trees and strings of bells moved by the wind. And when the men hear that sound, reflection on Buddha arises in them, reflection on the Law, reflection on the Church. With such arrays of excellences, &c.

"Now what do you think, O Sariputra, for what reason is that Tathagata called Amitayus? The length of life [ayus], O Sariputra, of that Tathagata and of those men there is immeasurable [amita]. There-

---

[5] Niraya, the hells, also called Naraka. Yamaloka, the realm of Yama, the judge of the dead, is explained as the four apayas, that is, Naraka, hell. [Translator's note.]

fore is that Tathagata called Amitayus, And ten kalpas have passed, O Sariputra, since that Tathagata awoke to perfect knowledge.

"And what do you think, O Sariputra, for what reason is that Tathagata called Amitabha? The splendour [abhâ], O Sariputra, of that Tathagata is unimpeded over all Buddha countries. Therefore is that Tathagata called Amitabha.

"And there is, O Sariputra, an innumerable assembly of disciples with that Tathagata, purified and venerable persons, whose number it is not easy to count. With such arrays of excellences, &c.

"And again, O Sariputra, of those beings also who are born in the Buddha country of the Tathagata Amitayus as purified Bodhisattvas, never to return again and bound by one birth only, of those Bodhisattvas also, O Sariputra, the number is not easy to count, except they are reckoned as infinite in number.

"Then again all beings, O Sariputra, ought to make fervent prayer for that Buddha country. And why? Because they come together there with such excellent men. Beings are not born in that Buddha country of the Tathagata Amitayus as a reward and result of good works performed in this present life. No, whatever son or daughter of a family shall hear the name of the blessed Amitayus, the Tathagata, and having heard it, shall keep it in mind, and with thoughts undisturbed shall keep it in mind for one, two, three, four, five, six or seven nights,—when that son or daughter of a family comes to die, then that Amitayus, the Tathagata, surrounded by an assembly of disciples and followed by a host of Bodhisattvas, will stand before them at their hour of death, and they will depart this life with tranquil minds. After their death they will be born in the world Sukhavatî, in the Buddha country of the same Amitayus, the Tathagata. Therefore, then, O Sariputra, having perceived this cause and effect, I with reverence say thus, Every son and every daughter of a family ought with their whole mind to make fervent prayer for that Buddha country. . . .

"Now what do you think, O Sariputra, for what reason is that repetition [treatise] of the Law called the Favour of all Buddhas? Every son or daughter of a family who shall hear the name of that repetition of the Law and retain in their memory the names of those blessed Buddhas, will be favoured by the Buddhas, and will never return again, being once in possession of the transcendent true knowledge. Therefore, then, O Sariputra, believe, accept, and do not doubt of me and those blessed Buddhas!

"Whatever sons or daughters of a family shall make mental prayer for the Buddha country of that blessed Amitayus, the Tathagata, or are making it now or have made it formerly, all these will never return again, being once in possession of the transcendent true knowledge. They will be born in that Buddha country, have been born, or are being born now. Therefore, then, O Sariputra, mental prayer is to be made for that Buddha country by faithful sons and daughters of a family.

"And as I at present magnify here the inconceivable excellences of those blessed Buddhas, thus, O Sariputra, do those blessed Buddhas magnify my own inconceivable excellences.

"A very difficult work has been done by Sakyamuni, the sovereign of the Sakyas. Having obtained the transcendent true knowledge in this world Saha, he taught the Law which all the world is reluctant to accept, during this corruption of the present kalpa,[6] during this corruption of mankind, during this corruption of belief, during this corruption of life, during this corruption of passions.

"This is even for me, O Sariputra, an extremely difficult work that, having obtained the transcendent true knowledge in this world Saha, I taught the Law which all the world is reluctant to accept, during this corruption of mankind, of belief, of passion, of life, and of this present kalpa."

Thus spoke Bhagavat joyful in his mind. And the honourable Sariputra, and the Bhikshus and Bodhisattvas, and the whole world with the gods, men, evil spirits and genii, applauded the speech of Bhagavat.

This is the Mahayanasutra
called Sukhavatî-vyuha.

---

[6] A cosmological unit of time, equal to 4.32 billion years.

12

Votive Inscription on a Silver
Plaque from Taxila

First–Second Centuries CE

---

*Mahayana Buddhism encouraged devotees to make contributions to mon-
asteries to secure their own nirvana and their welfare while on earth.
Many who did so had a record of their donation inscribed, so it would be
preserved. This inscription, on a silver plaque from Taxila, an ancient
town in Pakistan that was visited by Alexander the Great and later
became a Buddhist center, begins with the donor's identity. What does he
donate, and for what purpose? Notice his devotion to the Kushan ruler
and state, as well as to his own family.*

Anno 1.36, on the 15 day of the first month Ashadha, on this day were
established relics of the Lord by Urasaka, of the Imtavhria boys, the
Bactrian, the resident of the town of Noacha. By him these relics of the
Lord were established in his own bodhisattva chapel, in the Dharma-
rajika compound of Takshasila, for the bestowal of health on the Great
King, the King of Kings, the Son of Heaven, the Khushana, in honour of
all Buddhas, in honour of the Pratyekabuddhas, in honour of the Arhats,
in honour of all beings, in honour of mother and father, in honour of
friends, ministers, kinsmen, and blood-relations, for the bestowal of
health upon himself.

May this thy right munificence lead to Nirvana.

Kharoshthi Inscriptions, vol. 2, pt. 1, of the *Corpus Inscriptionum Indicrum*, ed. Sten
Konow (Varanasi: Indological Book House, 1969), 77.

4

The Oasis Towns of Central Asia and the Spread of Buddhism, Third–Seventh Centuries

13

Documents Excavated from the Ruins of Niya
Third Century

At Niya, a small oasis on the southern rim of the Takla Makan Desert that was once a major commercial center on the Silk Roads, archaeologists have excavated a Buddhist monastery with a stupa, or shrine, along with many documents in Chinese and Kharoshthi, an evolution of the Aramaic script that the Persians had brought to India. These documents reveal the monks' engagement in commercial transactions. Monks acted as witnesses and scribes for contracts and the arbitration of disputes, and the beneficiaries of their services sometimes paid them in rolls of silk. The monks accumulated so much silk that their regulations specified using rolls of silk to pay disciplinary fines. Together, the following documents suggest the interactions of people of many different ethnicities in an oasis town and the extent of Buddhist support of Silk Roads trade. What was the role of the Buddhist monastery in a small oasis community?

[Contract for the Sale of a Vineyard]

This document concerning a vineyard [bought] from Budhila and Budhaya is to be carefully preserved by [. . .] and Saṃgasri.

This is the seal of the monks Saṃca, Sujata, and Dhamila.

Thomas Burrow, *A Translation of the Kharoshthi Documents from Chinese Turkestan* (London: Royal Asiatic Society, 1940), 84–85, 60–61, 95.

In the 28th year, 11th month, 13th day in the reign of the great king Jitugha Amkvage, son of heaven, at this time Budhila and secondly Budhaya [two] of the sons of *śramaṃna* Athamo arose. They sold a vineyard of four *apcira*, and another piece of *letga kuthala* land in the *miṣi*-[land]. The whole amount is five [pieces of land]. Anamda bought it and paid the price, 1 golden stater and another 2 *muli*, and a later amount of 12 *muli*. They agreed on equal terms. It was well bought and well sold. This was written in the presence of the bhikṣu-sangha[1] at Cadota, at the request of Budhila and Budhaya. Witnesses were: the monk Budharachi, elder of the sangha, the monk Yipiya [. . .] the monk, and *dasavida* Samca, the monk Dhamamitra [. . .] the monk Dhama[kama], the servant of the reverend Ridhasena, Cigita, and the monks Tsagirsta and Sanaga. This was written at the command of the bhikṣu-sangha by me the scribe Apgeya, and at the command of Budhila and Budhaya. Its authority is for a thousand years, as long as life. Whoever at a future time shall bring up arguments [in an attempt] to alter it, he shall have no authority in front of the bhikṣu-sangha. The fine [for such an attempt] is five pieces of cloth, and the punishment [*dhaṃla* — danda] fifty strokes. Thus carefully [its] authority [is fixed]. There is no end.

The monk Budhavama and the monk Bhatra are witnesses.

[An Ownership Dispute about a Slave]

In the 4th year of his majesty the great King Mairi the son of heaven, on the 13th day of the 3rd month, at this date [?] the Supis[2] came to Calmadana; they plundered the kingdom and carried off the inhabitants. The Supis seized a man called Samrpina, a slave of the *vasu* Yonu[3] and sent him as a present to Cinaṣgaṣi [the Chinaman Ṣgaṣi]. Cinaṣgaṣi [provided] from here, as a recompense for the man, two golden staters and two drachmas. [Consequently] that man became the rightful property [?] of Ṣgaṣi. His own master, the *vasu* Yonu, did not wish to remove the man himself, and permission was given to Ṣgaṣi to sell him to others. Considering this Cinaṣgaṣi sold this man to Katge. As the price of the man [. . .] and one bow is right. Cinaṣgaṣi has sold well and Katge has bought well. From now on [. . .]

---

[1] A Buddhist monastery.
[2] A nomadic people who often attacked oases.
[3] A Greek, derived from Yona, from Ionia.

[Regulations for a Community of Monks]

In the 10th year of his majesty the great king, Jiṭugha Mahagiri, son of heaven, in the 12th month, 10th day [. . .] the community of monks in the capital laid down regulations for the community of monks in Cadota. It is heard that the novices do not pay attention to an elder, they disobey the old monks. Concerning this these regulations have been laid down by his majesty in front of the order of monks. The elders Silaprabha and Puṃnasena [are to be] in charge of the monastery [*viharavala*]. They have to administer all the activities of the community. [Disputes] are to be examined in accordance with the law. All the activities of the community of monks are to be administered by them [. . .] so that the community of monks shall be content in mind [*alanaṃna*]. Whichever monk does not partake in the activities of the community of monks shall pay a fine of one roll of silk. Whichever monk does not take part in the *posatha* ceremony, his penalty is [a fine of] one roll of silk. Whichever monk at the invitations to the *posatha* ceremony enters in householder's dress, shall pay a fine of one roll of silk. Whichever monk strikes another monk, [in the case of] a light [blow the fine is] five rolls of silk, [in the case of] a moderate [blow] ten rolls of silk, [in the case of] an excessive [blow] fifteen rolls of silk.

14

NANAI-VANDAK

Letter to the Noble Lord Varzakk

ca. 313

From the oasis towns of Sogdiana, between the Amu and Syr Rivers, many merchants traveled east to trade. One of them, Nanai-vandak, wrote from the Hexi Corridor (now in China's Gansu Province) to a friend and relative in Sogdiana. The letter never reached its destination and in 1907 was found by Aurel Stein, a British explorer and

Monks and Merchants: Silk Road Treasures from Northwest China, ed. Annette L. Juliano and Judith A. Lerner, trans. Nicholas Sims-Williams (New York: Harry N. Abrams, with the Asia Society, 2001), 49.

archaeologist, in the ruins of a watchtower on the Great Wall west of Dunhuang. It reveals a great deal about the nomadic invasions of China that disrupted trade and the commercial networks of Sogdian traders, including their financial transactions. Judging from this letter, how risky was it to carry out the long-distance trade along the Silk Road?

To the noble lord Varzakk son of Nanai-dhvar of the family Kanakk, 1,000 and 10,000 blessings and homage on bended knee, as is offered to the gods, sent by his servant Nanai-vandak. And, sirs, it would be a good day for him who might see you happy and free from illness; and, sirs, when I hear news of your good health, I consider myself immortal!

And, sirs, Armat-sach Jiuquan is safe and well and Arsach in Guzang is safe and well. And, sirs, it is three years since a Sogdian came from "inside."[1] I settled Ghotam-sach, and he is safe and well. He has gone to . . . and now no one comes from there so that I might write to you about the Sogdians who went "inside" how they fared and which countries they reached. And, sirs, the last emperor, so they say, fled from Luoyang because of the famine and fire was set to his palace and to the city, and the palace was burnt and the city [destroyed]. Luoyang is no more, Ye is no more! Moreover . . . as far as Ye (these same Huns [who] yesterday were the emperor's subjects! And, sirs, we do not know whether the remaining Chinese were able to expel the Huns [from] Changan, from China, or whether they took the country beyond. And [. . . in . . . there are] a hundred freemen from Samarkand . . . in . . . there are forty men. And, sirs, [. . . it is] three years since [. . . came] from "inside". . . .

And from Dunhuang up to Jincheng . . . to sell, linen cloth is going [=selling well?], and whoever has unmade cloth or woolen cloth . . .

And, sirs, as for us, whoever dwells in the region from Ji[ncheng] up to Dunhuang, we only survive so long as the . . . lives, and we are without family, old and on the point of death. If this were not so, [I would] not be ready to write to you about how we are. And, sirs, if I were to write to you everything about how China has fared, it would be beyond grief: there is no profit for you to gain from it. And, sirs, it is eight years since I sent Saghrak and Farn-aghat "inside" and it is three years since I received a reply from there. They were well . . . , but now, since the last evil occurred, I do [not] receive a reply from there about how they have

[1] Came from China.

fared. Moreover, four years ago I sent another man named Artikhu-vandak. When the caravan left Guzang, Wakhushakk . . . was there, and when they reached Luoyang . . . the Indians and the Sogdians there had all died of starvation. [And I] sent Nasyan to Dunhuang and he went "outside"[2] and entered Dunhuang, but now he has gone without permission from me, and he received a great retribution and was struck dead in the . . .

Lord Varzakk, my greatest hope is in your lordship! Pesakk son of Dhruwasp-vandak holds . . . staters of mine and he put it on deposit, not to be transferred, and you should hold it . . . sealed from now on, so that without my permission . . . Dhruwasp-vandak . . .

[Lord] Nanai-dhvar, you should remind Varzakk that he should withdraw this deposit, and you should both count it, and if the latter is to hold it you should add the interest to the capital and put it in a transfer document, and you should give this too to Varzakk. And if you think it fit that the latter should not hold it, then you should take it and give it to someone else whom you do think fit, so that this money may increase. And, behold, there is a certain orphan . . . and if he should live and reach adulthood, and he has no hope of anything other than this money, then, Nanai-dhvar, when it is heard that Takut has departed to the gods, the gods and my father's soul will be a support to you!, and when Takhsich-vandak is grown-up, give him a wife and do not send him away from you. . . . And when you need cash, then you should take 1,000 or 2,000 staters out of the money.

And Wan-razmak sent to Dunhuang for me 32 vesicles of musk belonging to Takut so that he might deliver them to you. When they are handed over you should make five shares, from which Takhsich-vandak should take three shares, and Pesakk should take one share, and you should take one share.

This letter was written when it was the year 13 of Lord Chirth-swan in the month Taghmich.

---

[2] Went out of China.

15

FAXIAN

A Record of the Buddhist Kingdoms

ca. 416

Around 399, Faxian, a Chinese Buddhist teacher, and several junior Buddhist monks set out on a pilgrimage to India to learn the true Buddhist doctrine. Faxian, who was about sixty years old at the time, was the first Chinese Buddhist to reach India. His party traveled through the oasis towns of the Takla Makan Desert and the rugged mountains of the Upper Indus Valley; on the way home, Faxian and the monks went by sea, stopping at a port in Southeast Asia. On his return to China, Faxian wrote a detailed account of his trip. In this passage, he describes Khotan, an oasis state on the southern edge of the Takla Makan Desert. To observe Khotan's famous Buddhist festival, Faxian and several others in the group remained there for three months, waiting for the festival to begin. Therefore, his description of this Silk Roads oasis is much more detailed than the descriptions of those he merely passed through. Once again the material wealth of Buddhist monasteries is confirmed. From Faxian's stay in Khotan, what can you infer is the significance of the oasis city on the Silk Road?

Having been on the road for one month and five days, we reached Khotan. This is a prosperous country, and the people there are affluent. They all follow Buddhist laws and enjoy playing and listening to Buddhist music. There are tens of thousands of monks, most of whom follow Mahayana teachings. All the monks receive food from public kitchens (and thus do not need to beg for food themselves). In this country people's homes are not all concentrated in one location (as in most of China), but are spread out at some distance from each other, and every household is marked by its own small stupa.[1] The smallest ones are about two *zhang* in height.[2] There is a Buddhist hostel for guest monks and other

[1] A tower housing relics of the Buddha.
[2] About twenty feet.

Faxian, *Faxian Zhuan Jiaozhu* [Faxian's Autobiography, Edited], ed. Zhang Xun (Shanghai: Guji Chubanshe, 1985), 13–14. Translated by Xinru Liu.

travelers. The king settled Faxian and his companions at a Sangharama. This Sangharama, called Gomati, is a Mahayana monastery. The sound of a gong summons the three thousand monks to their meals. All enter the dining hall ceremonially and sit down in a designated order. The entire hall is totally in silence; even the noise made by vessels is absent. When a monk wants a servant to add more food, he does not call out to him, but raises his hand to summon him.

Huijing, Daozheng, and Huida proceeded to Jiecha Guo [Tashkurgan?], but Faxian and others decided to stay for three months so that they could observe the parade of the Buddha statues.

There are fourteen large monasteries and numerous small ones in the country. On the first day of the fourth month, the people of the city start by sweeping the streets and decorating its lanes. A huge, heavily decorated tent is pitched on top of the city gate, where the king, the queen, and the palace women take up residence. Since Gomati monastery follows the Mahayana doctrine, which is the king's favorite school, its monks march first in the parade. The monastery is about three or four *li*[3] from the city. A four-wheeled wagon is used to support a superstructure as tall as three zhang, and this framework holds the statues. The wagon looks like a moving palace, decorated with the Seven Treasures,[4] silk banners, and canopies. A statue of the Buddha stands in the wagon, attended by two bodhisattvas. Heavenly beings, carved and then enameled with golden and silver materials, are hanging above the Buddha. When the wagon stopped a hundred steps from the city gate, the king came out of the gate from a side door to meet the Buddha statue. He took off his crown and put on a new set of clothes. Holding flowers and bundles of incense, the king walked barefoot to meet the Buddha. He touched the feet of the Buddha with his head, then spread the flowers and burned the incense. When the wagon proceeded through the gate, the queen and palace women strewed flowers from above. Every monastery provided a different, but also beautifully decorated array of wagons and statues. It took a whole day for one monastery to parade its statues. Having started on the first day of the month, the parade finished on the fourteenth day. After the parade was over, the king and queen returned to their palace. . . .

The kings of the six states east of the Pamir Plateau give all of their precious belongings away to support Buddhism. Humans hardly ever enjoy such things themselves.

[3] About two miles.
[4] A sacred combination of seven gems and other precious materials that Buddhists donate to the Buddha in order to receive merits in their next life.

16

SONG YUN AND HUISHENG

The Mission of Song Yun and Huisheng
ca. 547

In 518 the Northern Wei empress dowager sent two Buddhist monks, Song Yun and Huisheng, to India to make a pilgrimage on behalf of the royal family. They took many treasures, including silk banners and incense pouches, to donate to Buddhist establishments on the way, and they made a record of the treasures received and owned by these monasteries. Their record is preserved only because it was included by Yang Xuanzhi in his Buddhist Monasteries in Luoyang, *a book that blamed the collapse of the Northern Wei on the rulers' patronage of Buddhism and the extravagance of Buddhist monasteries. The following excerpts describe Song Yun and Huisheng's encounter with the ruler and peoples of Khotan and with a group of nomads called Yeda—Hephthalites in Western records—as well as their destination, Gandhara, a Buddhist land then under nomadic rule. Notice the descriptions of the customs and dress of these peoples. What evidence do you find of the exchange of goods and ideas on the Silk Roads?*

In the neighborhood of Wenyili,[1] there was a house in which a man known as Song Yun resided. He was from Dunhuang and had once accompanied the monk Huisheng on a trip to the Western Regions. In the eleventh month of the first year of the Shengui era,[2] the empress dowager had sent Huisheng, who was then one of the monks at Chongli Monastery, to the Western Regions in order to acquire Buddhist scriptures. His expedition brought back 170 different kinds of scriptures, and all of them are wonderful Mahayana texts.

[1] In the city of Luoyang.
[2] 518.

Yang Xuanzhi, *Luoyang Qielan Ji* [Buddhist Monasteries in Luoyang] (Shanghai: Guji Chubanshi, 1978), 251–52, 271, 288–89, 317–18, 329. Translated by Xinru Liu.

They had departed from the capital city of Luoyang and then traveled for forty days before reaching Chiling,[3] which was located on the Northern Wei's westernmost border and was the site of an imperial military garrison. . . .

In the state of Yutian,[4] the king wears a gold crown shaped like the red comb on a rooster's head. Hanging behind it is a piece of silk two *chi*[5] long and five *cun*[6] wide. His honor guards carry a drum, a bugle, a golden gong, a bow and arrows, two halberds, and five spears. No fewer than one hundred royal guards carrying knives stand around him. Women in this country wear trousers, tighten their blouses with belts, and gallop on horses just like men. The people there cremate their dead and build Buddhist stupas over the buried bones. Mourners cut their hair and scar their faces to express their grief. After their hair grows back to a length of four cun, they return to their usual routine. The only body that is not cremated is the body of the king, which is put in a coffin and buried in the wild, where a temple is then built for carrying out sacrificial ceremonies. . . .

By the beginning of the tenth month of the year, they entered the territory of the Yeda.[7] Mountains and lakes were spread out on a vast landscape. The people do not live in walled cities. Instead, they live like nomads. They build their homes out of felt and often move their tents in order to find ample amounts of water and grass.[8] They move to cool places in the summer and warm locations in the winter. They are not literate, do not practice any rites, and do not have any formal education. They do not understand the cosmological cycles at all. In their rough version of a calendar, they count twelve months as a year, and every month is the same length. There is no leap year in their calendar. They receive tribute from many countries, as far south as Dieluo,[9] as far north as the Turks, as far east as Yutian, and as far west as Persia. As many as forty-some states come to pay tribute to them on ritual occasions. The king sits in a large felt tent about forty square *bu*[10] in area and the walls of the tent are covered with woolen rugs. The king wears a robe made

---

[3] Now Mount Riyala in Qinghai Province.
[4] Khotan, an oasis city on the southern rim of the Takla Makan Desert.
[5] A *chi* is roughly one foot.
[6] A *cun* is roughly one inch.
[7] "The territory of the Yeda" was better known as Tukharistan. It was located in what is now northern Afghanistan.
[8] Water and grass for their livestock.
[9] Not identified.
[10] *Bu* is a loosely used unit, about two yards in length, which means the tent was about 160 square yards.

of silk brocade and sits on a golden chair that has four golden feet in the shape of phoenixes. Knowing that the ambassador had come from China's Great Wei Empire, the Yeda king knelt down twice to express his homage after he received the imperial edict. When the king provides a banquet for his guests, there is one man who loudly announces that the guests can come in, and when it is over, he loudly announces that it has ended. That is the only ritual associated with the banquet, and there is no such thing as musical performances. The queen of Yeda also wears a silk brocade robe which is so long that three chi of it would have been dragging across the floor were it not for the servant who followed her and held it up off the floor. She wears an eight-chi-long scarf that is folded into the shape of a cone, and attached on top of this scarf is a three-chi-long horn that is beautifully decorated with colored jade. The queen rides in a carriage whenever she goes outside, and in the tent she sits on a golden chair supported by four legs, and the bottom of each leg is shaped like the six-tusked white elephant[11] as well as a lion. When she moves, the wives of major ministers hold up her parasol. It appears that these women also wear a kind of cone-shaped scarf that hangs down and has a round shape like a parasol. After observing their outfits, one noticed that they too mark their status in the hierarchy by their apparel and their adornments. Among all the barbarians, they are the superpower. They do not believe in Buddhism, but worship many gods. They slaughter animals and eat raw meat, with utensils made out of the Seven Treasures.[12] The tribute gifts that come from countries subject to their power are numerous and precious and often are rarities. The country of Yeda is about twenty thousand li[13] from the Chinese capital at Luoyang. . . .

In the middle of the fourth month of the first year in the Zhengguang era,[14] they entered the country of Gandhara.[15] Its landscape is similar to that of Uddiyana,[16] and its former name was Yeboluo. The country also has been conquered by the Yeda, who established a teqin[17] as a

---

[11] The six-tusked white elephant was an incarnation of the Buddha in one of his former lives.

[12] A sacred combination of seven gems and other precious materials that Buddhists donate to the Buddha in order to receive merits in their next life.

[13] About ten thousand kilometers or six thousand miles.

[14] 520.

[15] The region around Peshawar and Taxila in what is now northern Pakistan.

[16] In Pakistan's Swat Valley.

[17] The title of a chief in the Turkish language. It appears that the Yeda (Hephthalites) borrowed this title from a Turkish neighbor or appointed a Turkish chief as the ruler of Gandhara.

king. Now a second-generation teqin is ruling the country. He is cruel in nature and has killed many people. He does not believe in Buddhism, but makes sacrifices to demons and other deities. The people in the country belong to the Brahman caste and have faith in Buddhism, and read its scriptures all the time. They are really unhappy about being ruled by this king. The king considers himself brave and powerful, and therefore he has been engaged in a territorial war with Jibin[18] for three years now. On the battlefield, the king deploys seven hundred war elephants, with ten soldiers on each elephant carrying knives and forks. Knives also are bound to the tusks of the war elephants in order to attack his enemies. He spends most of his time on the frontier and rarely comes back to the center to run the country. The troops are tired, and people are exhausted and complain a lot. . . .

When Huisheng left the capital in Luoyang, the empress dowager had entrusted him with one thousand banners. Each was made of multicolored silk and was a hundred chi in length.[19] She also gave him five hundred brocade bags for incense. Princes and courtiers also contributed two thousand [silk] banners. From Yutian to Gandhara, Huisheng had donated these gifts to each of the Buddhist shrines and ceremonial locations that he encountered. Among the gifts of the empress dowager, the only thing he had left was one banner of one hundred chi, which Huisheng had saved for the stupa of King Sibi.[20] Song Yun also donated two slaves, one man and a woman, to the Queli Stupa, so that they could sweep and clean the stupa. Huisheng, meanwhile, hired skilled artisans to copy the image of the Queli Stupa and the illustrated stories of the Shakyamuni[21] on the four major stupas, and he used some savings from his travel fund to pay for these expenses.

[18] In Kashmir, north of India and Pakistan.
[19] About thirty yards.
[20] A wise king mentioned in the Buddhist *Jataka*, stories that illuminate the previous lives of the Buddha.
[21] Another name for Buddha. Literally, the wise man of the Shakya people.

17

HUILI AND YANZONG

The Life of Xuanzang

ca. 664–688

Xuanzang, called the Dharma Master by his disciples, was a Chinese Buddhist monk who made a pilgrimage to India. He began his trip in 629, when the newly established Tang dynasty was at war with the Western Turks, a nomadic tribe then located near China's western frontier. Although the Chinese court had forbidden any traffic across this border, Xuanzang persevered on his journey, eventually reaching India and then returning to China. He made detailed observations on the geography, climate, and customs of every country he traveled through. Several decades later, two of his disciples, Huili and Yanzong, wrote a biography of Xuanzang. They included personal details of his journey to India based on what they heard from the teacher and what they observed of his career in China. The following passages record Xuanzang's experience in the oasis state of Gaochang and his meeting with the Yabgu Khan, a Turkish chief who held hegemonic power over Central Asia on the steppe and in the oasis towns of the deserts from the Chinese border to the Aral Sea. Xuanzang was impressed by the material culture that he observed in the territories of this steppe ruler. What does this account reveal about Chinese attitudes toward the people of oasis towns and the nomads of the steppe?

[Gaochang]

On the next day, the king had a huge tent pitched to open the lecture series. More than three hundred people were seated in the tent. The queen mother and palace women, and the king with his generals and ministers, were seated in their own sectors of the tent to attend my lectures. At the beginning of every lecture, the king came out to meet the Dharma Master, holding the incense burner. When the two reached the Dharma throne, the king knelt down for the Dharma Master to step on

Huili and Yanzong, *Daciensi Sanzangfashi Zhuan* [Biography of Xuanzang, the Dharma Teacher of the Great Monastery of Compassion], ed. Sun Yutang and Xie Fang (Beijing: Zhonghua Shuju, 1983), 21, 27–28. Translated by Xinru Liu.

his back to ascend to the throne. In this way the Master lectured every day [for a month].

After the lecture series, the king recruited four novice monks to attend the Dharma Master. The king had thirty sets of liturgical clothes made for the Dharma Master. Because the weather in the Western Lands was cold, the king had several sets of face covers, gloves, boots, socks, and other accessories made. He provided one hundred *liang*[1] of gold, thirty thousand silver coins, five hundred bolts of silk damask, silk tabby, and other silk weaving textiles. The gift was intended to pay for a round trip expenses to India and a stay all together for twenty years. He also provided thirty horses and twenty-five laborers to accompany the Master. The head officer of his palace would accompany the Master to the headquarters of the Yabgu Khan, the king of the Western Turks. The king wrote twenty-four letters—every letter was attached to a bolt of heavy damask—to Kucha and other oasis states on the road to the west. He also prepared a special package of gifts for Yabgu Khan, including five hundred bolts of damask and other light weave and two carts of fruits. His letter to Yabgu Khan says: "The Dharma Master is your humble slave's brother who wants to go to the Brahman Country[2] to learn the Dharma. May your highness Khan protect the Dharma Master in the same way as you protect your humble slave. Also please order the states to the west to provide postal horse service to send him to cross the border [of your territory]." . . .

[Yabgu Khan]

Emerging from the snow mountains, the Dharma Master saw a great, clear lake. The circumference of the lake was from fourteen hundred to fifteen hundred *li*.[3] It was elongated in shape, the length of north-south direction being shorter than that of the east-west direction. On the bank of the lake, one sees only waves of water. Even when wind is still, the waves are as high as a few *zhangs*.[4] Following the coast of the lake to the northwest, in about five hundred li, the Dharma Master reached Suyab city, where the Dharma Master came upon Yabgu Khan, who was on his hunting trip with a large horde of horse-riding warriors. Wearing a robe of green damask, exposing his hair, the khan bound his head with

[1] One *liang* is approximately 150 ounces.
[2] India.
[3] The circumference was between three hundred and four hundred miles.
[4] One *zhang* is about three yards.

a piece of white silk about one zhang in length. The two hundred or so advanced officials [*Daguan*] surrounding him all wore robes of colorful brocade and braided their hair. All lower officers and soldiers wore fur and wool, holding spikes with oxtail brooms and arches. There were so many camels and horses that one could not see the end of the horde. Receiving his greetings, the khan was delighted, saying: "I am right in the middle of my hunting trip and will be back to my palace soon. You, Dharma Master, please go ahead to my place and wait for me." He thus ordered Damazhi, an advanced official, to escort the Master to his head-quarters to settle in.

The khan took another three days to return, and he summoned the Dharma Master to an audience. The khan lived in a great tent, deco-rated with golden ornaments. Its splendor was so dazzling that it caused people to wince. All advanced officials were seated on two long rugs, and their brocade silk attire was impressive. Guards stood behind them. As he looked around, the Dharma Master thought that even though the khan was only a nomadic king, his court was quite elegant.

When the Dharma Master was about thirty steps outside the khan's tent, the khan came out to meet him. After exchanging greetings through interpreters, they both were seated. As fire worshippers, the Turks did not sit on wooden chairs because wood embodies fire. They all sat on heavy cushions, but set up an iron cross-leg chair covered with cushions for the Dharma Master. Soon a Chinese envoy and a Gaochang envoy were led in with official letters and gifts. The khan examined the gifts and was very pleased. He asked them to be seated and ordered wine served and music played. The khan, his ministers, and the envoys drank wine, and grape juice was served to the Dharma Master. Thus, all urged others to drink; wine was poured into bowls and goblets, accom-panied by musical melodies of various styles of the region. Even though the music was not Chinese, it was quite pleasing to the senses and feel-ings. After a short while, food was served; cooked fresh lamb and veal were set in front of the people. They made special vegetarian food for the Dharma Master, including pancakes, cream, crystal sugar, honey, grapes, and so forth. After they ate, they again filled the cups with grape juice for the Dharma Master, asking him to lecture on Dharma. The Dharma Master thus taught them the "Ten Virtues concerning com-passionate lives," and the *Paramita* [the way of transferring to] libera-tion. After the lecture, the khan raised his hand to his forehead, happily accepting the teaching.

The Dharma Master stayed with the khan for several days. The khan tried to persuade the Master to stay there: "You, Master, do not need to go to India. That place is very hot, the weather in the tenth month[5] is similar to that of the fifth month[6] here. Looking at your complexion, I am afraid your body cannot take that heat. People there are dark in skin and undignified, that is, not good looking." The Dharma Master replied: "I want to go there to look for the sacred tracks of the Buddha and learn the Dharma." The khan therefore searched in his troop for one who understood Chinese and other languages. A young man who had been in Chang'an for several years and learned Chinese was made the interpreting officer. The khan had several state official letters written, and he ordered the interpreting officer to escort the Dharma Master to Kapisa.[7] He also provided a liturgical robe made of red damask and fifty bolts of plain silk. The khan and his ministers marched more than ten li to see the Dharma Master off.

[5] November.
[6] June.
[7] Begram, in Afghanistan.

18

Inventories Excavated from a Turfan Cemetery

Mid-Seventh Century

During the first half of the seventh century, a new kind of inventory began to appear in Central Asian graves. Near Turfan, an important station on the Silk Roads, archaeologists have found written contracts made with the gods and buried with the deceased. These contracts include an inventory of the goods that the deceased was offering to the gods. Rather than being placed in the graves, the goods were presumably given to various Buddhist institutions, thereby providing the deceased with merits that would aid in the next life. Some inventories recorded the good deeds that the deceased had performed; these, too, would bestow merits and help ensure a good position in the next life. The inventories help modern

National Bureau of Antiquaries, *Tulufan Chutu Wenshu* [Documents Excavated from Turfan] (Beijing: Wenwu Chubanshe, 1983), 4:32–33, 7:66–74. Translated by Xinru Liu.

readers envision the funeral rites performed by Buddhist monks and the variety of goods received by Buddhist institutions. In the inventories, can you find items that would be used in daily life, or commodities that could have been traded for profit?

Tang Zhuanghui, ca. 641

One set of silk damask blouse and pants, one set of fine silk shirt and pants, a pair of brocade covered boots

One *jiaoju* [?] belt, one white silk scarf, one bundle of white cotton cloth, one knife with a buffalo horn handle

One red robe, one crown decorated with a dragon, one white silk shirt, one set of white silk shirt and pants

One pillow in the shape of a cock, one face cover made of Persian brocade, one set of goggles with lenses of silver sieve, one jade container for the "climbing to heaven" silk rope[1]

One thousand pieces of white silk, ten thousand pieces of variously colored silks, an abundant amount of gold and silver

One set of bow and arrows in a bottle gourd container, a piece of the climbing to heaven silk rope as long as 100,009,000 *zhang*[2]

[My soul] wants to go either to the far end of the east sea, or to the far end of the west sea. Witnessed by Zhang Jiangu and recorded by Li Dingdu, thus no one should stop me [from disposing of these belongings in this way].

Please follow the law and the statute!

Xinfu, 672

Please note:

These are the merits accumulated by my father-in-law[3] when he was alive. After he became ill last year, he did the following meritorious things.

On the twenty-third day of the twelfth month, he invited twenty monks to recite Buddhist sutras, and at the same time he donated a horse to

---

[1] An imaginary rope the deceased could use to climb up to heaven.

[2] Approximately 300,027,000 yards, or roughly 170,480 miles.

[3] *Xinfu* means "new bride," so the writer of this inventory is a young and faithful daughter-in-law.

the Buddha. He [also donated] one set of yellow silk damask robes and skirts in order to confess his sins and obtain remission of them.

On the first day of the first month of this year, he invited ten Buddhist monks to turn [the wheel of] sutras[4] every day until the eve of the seventh day. On that day, in addition, he invited fifty monks to recite sutras and donated one silver plate weighing twenty *liang*[5] to the monastery, and on that same day he made a confession and received a remission of his sins.

After the eighth day of the first month, he invited ten monks to turn [the wheel of] sutras through the eighteenth day, [which means] altogether [?] spins of the *Great Prajna* [?] Sutra [Diamond Sutra].

On the thirteenth day of the first month, he invited twenty nuns and monks to recite sutras and made a confession and received a remission of his sins.

My elder brother[6] at Anxi has burned incense and made wishes [on his behalf]. At the same time he invited Fosheng, the Teacher of Meditation, to read the *Vajna Prajna* [?] Sutra a thousand times [?]. That day he also provided a vegetarian feast for the monks, who then recited various sutras for six [?], and he went to confession. [He] also offered, [in front of] many people, eighty rolls of silk so that a mural portraying Vimalakirlti,[7] Manjusri,[8] and other bodhisattvas could be painted on the southern wall of the Buddha Hall in the Beitian Monastery at Anxi. Please be advised that he also pledged that he would contribute additional merits on his father's behalf.

On the seventh day of the second month, ten monks and nuns were invited to [hear his confession] and remit his sins.

During the night of the seventh day, on the night before my father-in-law passed away, he made an oath to donate to the Matreya Buddha Monastery, Xuanjue Si, a large, seven *hu*[9] white lion [sculpture] as its permanent property. A hundred monks were invited to recite sutras and two monks were invited to perform rituals for seven days. A forty-nine

---

[4] Buddhists believe that the recitation of sutras by the monks creates many merits for the patron who sponsors the performance. They also believe that turning a stone wheel on which the words of the sutra are carved is tantamount to the sutra's being recited by humans. Thus the turning of the carved wheel is a mechanical way to repeat sutras many times, thereby creating many merits for the patron.

[5] About twenty-six ounces.

[6] The elder brother is most likely the writer's husband, who had been assigned to an official position at Anxi and thus was not home at the time. Chinese women call their husbands or lovers "elder brother," and men call their wives or lovers "younger sisters."

[7] A lay Buddhist sage.

[8] The bodhisattva of wisdom.

[9] About 70 liters or 18.5 gallons. A *hu* is a unit for measuring grains.

chi,[10] five-colored banner was made. On the eighth day, after serving a vegetarian feast, according to the wishes made by my father-in-law, many people were invited to witness the donation of the large sculpture, the white lion. Luotong the Dharma Teacher was invited to receive his confession and to remit his sins. Thereafter Luotong the Dharma Teacher was invited to ordain my father-in-law as a bodhisattva. And again he made his confession.

Please note.

On the eighth day, after the gathering of people had dispersed, Meng the Meditation Teacher was invited to hear his oath of practicing Buddhism. By the second hour of early morning, the confession was made. At that time, my father-in-law donated a pair of double-layer silk trousers to two monks carrying out the ceremony. He soon passed away [on the evening of the eighth day]. Immediately a yellow banner was made, with a copy of the *Sutra of Happy Rebirth* on it. The banner was taken to the monastery to be hung there. Forty-nine lamps were also lit there in the morning and in the evening. Two monks performed a rehearsal of the confession for my father-in-law while the lamps were lit. Meanwhile, three monks were reciting [?] sutras. My father-in-law deserves to be reborn in any of the pure lands located in all ten regions of the universe.

The divine banner that is forty-nine chi in length, ordered by my father-in-law before he passed away, was ready yesterday. It will be displayed on the seventh ceremonial day.

Please be advised.

Yesterday I returned to the stupa where I found a note behind the gate that was handwritten by my father-in-law, saying that he still needs to have the one hundred volumes of the *Nirvana Sutra* recited an additional two and half times to complete his virtuous work. I thus invited the verger of the monastery, Zhang the Meditation Teacher, to recite half time the twenty volumes of the *Nirvana Sutra*. I also invited him to recite one set of the *Lotus Sutra* [*Saddharmapundarika*] and one set of the *Golden Light Sutra*. The seventh-day ritual [ceremony] was performed, and [?] a monk recited forty volumes of the *Nirvana Sutra* once and provided [my father-in-law] a remission of his sins. Since the seventh day of the month, during which time the lamps have been lit in the morning and in the evening for the remission of his sins, two monks have been invited to recite sutras continuously, without interruption.

---

[10] About fifty feet long.

By the twenty-first day of this month, forty monks had been invited to do one recitation of the forty volumes of the *Nirvana Sutra*. Adding all the performances together, the *Nirvana Sutra* has thus been recited [two] and half times [a hundred volumes in all].

Today the *Nirvana Sutra* is being recited again, and the following items are being donated to the Buddhist Three Treasures.[11]

A horse is for the Buddha
A set of saddles is for the Dharma
One robe made of yellow silk brocade
One silk scarf
One blouse made of yellow cloth
One man's hair cover made of silk crepe
One blouse made of black cloth
One half-sleeved blouse made of plain silk damask
One long-sleeved blouse made of rough silk
One belt made of refined copper
One knife with a handle made of *chenxiang*[12] and a gold-covered rim.
One pair of boots with felt
One boot connecting band [?] made of two-colored silk damask
One pair of double-layer pants made of white silk
One pair of white silk pants
One white silk shirt
One pair of white silk pants
One pair of fine silk stockings
One skirt made of dark green silk damask
One belly cover [*mofu?*] made of purple and yellow striped gauze
One red silk gauze shawl
One purple silk damask jacket hemmed with brocade
A pair of five-colored embroidered silk shoes
One pair of dark green silk damask stockings with brocade band

The donation of these goods has been witnessed by the above mentioned gathering.

One skirt made of double-layer purple silk damask
Two shawls of double-layer green damask
One double-layer shirt of skin colored silk

---

[11] The Three Treasures are the Buddha, the *sangha,* and the dharma.
[12] *Aquilaria agallocha*, a fragrant tropical wood.

The above goods have been donated by the new bride [myself] for
my father-in-law.

All the goods listed here were donated to the Buddhist Three
Treasures on the twenty-second day of the second month of this
year, in front of a gathering of people.

Please be advised.

When my father-in-law was ill, he donated a bundle of silk floss to
Meng the Meditation Teacher for reciting the *Golden Light Sutra* to the
various heavenly gods.

Please be advised.

Message to my father-in-law:

*I have carefully checked and recorded here all the merits you accumu-
lated during your life. All the merits added under your name after you
had passed away have also been listed here. Please take this inventory of
merits with you to confirm them in the future. Please try to be reborn into
the divinely pure lands of Buddha instead of seeking to be reborn into this
world where one still goes through rebirth cycles. The estate, including all
the land, gardens, houses, wives, sons, daughters, slaves, servants, and so
forth, are illusions, and not one of them is real. Father, you were constantly reading Buddhist sutras and studying their meaning, so you should
understand this truth. It is only because the paths of the living and the dead
lead in different directions that I am afraid that [after your departure]
you have become confused. You were ordained [as a bodhisattva] at the
moment of your departure, plus you have so many accumulated merits.
These are all good reasons that you should try to move up and strive to get
into a better place to be reborn. Please do not descend to the low places of
this world due to your attachment to your loved ones.*

*I have honestly recorded [your meritorious behavior] and provided all
the details, big and small. Please leave the Three Realms[13] and ascend to
the Supreme Realm.*

*Whatever category of rebirth you enter, please let us know by sending us
a message in our dreams.*

---

[13] The Three Realms are earth, atmosphere, and heaven.

5

The Byzantine Empire and Silks in Royal Purple, Sixth–Ninth Centuries

---

19

PROCOPIUS

History of the Wars

ca. 550

Procopius (d. ca. 565) was a historian and military commander during the reign of Justinian, and his History of the Wars *is primarily an account of Justinian's campaigns against the barbarian states in the west and the Persians in the east. In the first passage, Procopius credits Justinian with introducing sericulture to the west, but like other historians who focused on kings and heroes, he neglects the specifics of technology. The Byzantines would have first needed to learn to cultivate a particular variety of mulberry tree and to nurture the silkworms. In the absence of mature mulberry groves in Byzantium, the "smuggled" silkworms would have starved to death, even if the eggs had somehow managed to survive the long journey from China. In addition, unraveling the cocoon's long filament is a highly skilled process not easily acquired. Perhaps Procopius simplified the complicated process of technology transfer in the interest of glorifying his emperor. In the second passage, Procopius describes the*

---

arrival of bubonic plague in Constantinople in 542, an outbreak so severe that more than one-third of the city's population perished. This account is a reminder that diseases, too, traveled the Silk Roads. In 1347–1351, up to half the population of Europe would die when another wave of the deadly plague arrived from Asia. According to the History of the Wars, *what role did Emperor Justinian play in the lives of his people?*

[Sericulture]

At about this time certain monks, coming from India and learning that the Emperor Justinian entertained the desire that the Romans should no longer purchase their silk from the Persians, came before the emperor and promised so to settle the silk question that the Romans would no longer purchase this article from their enemies, the Persians, nor indeed from any other nation; for they had, they said, spent a long time in the country situated north of the numerous nations of India — a country called Serinda[1] — and there they had learned accurately by what means it was possible for silk to be produced in the land of the Romans. Whereupon the emperor made very diligent enquiries and asked them many questions to see whether their statements were true, and the monks explained to him that certain worms are the manufacturers of silk, nature being their teacher and compelling them to work continually. And while it was impossible to convey the worms thither alive, it was still practicable and altogether easy to convey their offspring. Now the offspring of these worms, they said, consisted of innumerable eggs from each one. And men bury these eggs, long after the time when they are produced, in dung, and, after thus healing them for a sufficient time, they bring forth the living creatures. After they had thus spoken, the emperor promised to reward them with large gifts and urged them to confirm their account in action. They then once more went to Serinda and brought back the eggs to Byzantium, and in the manner described caused them to be transformed into worms, which they fed on the leaves of the mulberry; and thus they made possible from that time forth the production of silk in the land of the Romans. At that time then matters stood thus between the Romans and the Persians, both as touching the war and in regard to silk. . . .

---

[1] Serinda is the land between China (Seres) and India, more specifically the deserts and oases of Central Asia.

[The Plague]

It started from the Aegyptians who dwell in Pelusium. Then it divided and moved in one direction towards Alexandria and the rest of Aegypt, and in the other direction it came to Palestine on the borders of Aegypt; and from there it spread over the whole world, always moving forward and travelling at times favourable to it. For it seemed to move by fixed arrangement, and to tarry for a specified time in each country, casting its blight slightingly upon none, but spreading in either direction right out to the ends of the world, as if fearing lest some corner of the earth might escape it. For it left neither island nor cave nor mountain ridge which had human inhabitants; and if it had passed by any land, either not affecting the men there or touching them in indifferent fashion, still at a later time it came back; then those who dwelt round about this land, whom formerly it had afflicted most sorely, it did not touch at all, but it did not remove from the place in question until it had given up its just and proper tale of dead, so as to correspond exactly to the number destroyed at the earlier time among those who dwelt round about. And this disease always took its start from the coast, and from there went up to the interior. And in the second year it reached Byzantium in the middle of spring, where it happened that I was staying at that time. And it came as follows. . . . With the majority it came about that they were seized by the disease without becoming aware of what was coming either through a waking vision or a dream. And they were taken in the following manner. They had a sudden fever, some when just roused from sleep, others while walking about, and others while otherwise engaged, without any regard to what they were doing. And the body shewed no change from its previous colour, nor was it hot as might be expected when attacked by a fever, nor indeed did any inflammation set in; but the fever was of such a languid sort from its commencement and up till evening that neither to the sick themselves nor to a physician who touched them would it afford any suspicion of danger. It was natural, therefore, that not one of those who had contracted the disease expected to die from it. But on the same day in some cases, in others on the following day, and in the rest not many days later, a bubonic swelling developed; and this took place not only in the particular part of the body which is called "boubon,"[2] that is, below the abdomen, but also inside the armpit, and in some cases also beside the ears, and at different points on the thighs. . . .

[2] Groin. [Translator's note.]

Now the disease in Byzantium ran a course of four months, and its greatest virulence lasted about three. And at first the deaths were a little more than the normal, then the mortality rose still higher, and afterwards the tale of dead reached five thousand each day, and again it even came to ten thousand and still more than that. . . . Such was the course of the pestilence in the Roman empire at large as well as in Byzantium. And it fell also upon the land of the Persians and visited all the other barbarians besides.

20

PROCOPIUS

The Secret History

ca. 550

In addition to writing his official history of Justinian's reign, Procopius also wrote a secret history that reveals what he really thought of the emperor. This document was discovered much later in the Vatican Library and was first published in 1623. In this passage, Procopius describes Justinian's manipulation of the silk industry and the effects of his driving private dealers out of the silk market. How does the view of Justinian here differ from that in the History of the Wars*? What does* The Secret History *suggest about the purpose and accuracy of court histories generally?*

But when these sovereigns had brought most of the merchandise under the control of the monopolies,[1] as they are called, and every single day were strangling those who wished to buy anything, and only the shops where clothing is sold were left untouched by them, they devised this scheme for that business also. Garments made of silk had been wont from ancient times to be produced in the cities of Beirut and Tyre in

[1] Here Procopius refers to state control of tariff and coinage.

Procopius, *The Anecdota or Secret History*, trans. H. B. Dewing (Cambridge, Mass.: Harvard University Press, 1935), 297–301.

Phoenicia. And the merchants and craftsmen and artisans of these stuffs had lived there from ancient times, and this merchandise was carried thence to the whole world. And when, in the reign of Justinian, those engaged in this trade both in Byzantium and in the other cities were selling this fabric at an excessive price, excusing themselves with the statement that at the time in question they were paying the Persians a higher price than formerly, and that the customs-houses were now more numerous in the land of the Romans, the Emperor gave everyone the impression that he was vexed with this, and he made a general provision by law that one pound of this stuff should not cost more than eight gold pieces. And the penalty appointed for those who should transgress this law was to be deprived of all the money they had. This seemed to the people altogether impossible and out of the question. For it was not possible for the importing merchants, having bought these cargoes at a higher price, to sell them to the dealers for less. Therefore they no longer cared to engage in the importation of this stuff, and they gradually disposed of the remainder of their cargoes by rather furtive methods, selling no doubt to certain of the notables who found a satisfaction in making a shew of such finery through the lavish expenditure of their money—or, in a certain sense, they were obliged to do so. And when the Empress[2] became aware of these transactions through the whisperings of certain persons, though she did not investigate the gossip that was going round, she immediately took the entire cargoes away from the men and, in addition, imposed upon them a fine of a centenarium of gold. . . . But this particular business is under the control, among the Romans at least, of the official in charge of the imperial treasures. Consequently, having appointed Peter surnamed Barsymes to this position, not long afterwards, they indulged him in doing execrable things. For while he required all other men strictly to observe the law, the craftsmen of this trade he required to work for himself alone, and he would sell dyes, no longer furtively but in the public square of the marketplace, at the rate of no less than six gold pieces the ounce for the ordinary quality, but more than twenty-four gold pieces for the imperial dye which they are wont to call *holoverum*. And while he produced large sums from that source for the Emperor, he himself gained still more without being observed, and this practice, which began with him, has always continued. For he alone, up to the present time, is established, with no attempt at concealment, as both importer and retailer of this merchandise. Consequently the importers who in former times had engaged in this trade both at Byzantium and in the other cities, on sea

---

[2] Empress Theodora, Justinian's queen.

and on land, now had to endure, as was to be expected, the hardships arising from this procedure. And in the other cities practically the whole population found itself suddenly reduced to beggary. For the mechanics and the hand-workers were naturally compelled to struggle with hunger, and many in consequence changed their citizenship and went off as fugitives to the land of Persia. But always the Master of the Treasures stood alone as sole manager of this business, and while he did consent to deliver to the Emperor a portion of its profits, as has been said, he carried off the greater portion for himself and was enriching himself through public calamities. So much then for this.

21

The Book of the Eparch
ca. 895

The eparch *(mayor) of Constantinople was the guardian of the imperial monopoly on many high-end luxuries. During the reign of Emperor Leo VI (886–912),* The Book of the Eparch *listed regulations for artisan and merchant guilds. Silk manufacturers were among the most closely supervised. Even though the Byzantines had to import silk material from foreign sources after the Muslim caliphates took control of the lands of the mulberry groves, the artisans and merchants dealing with raw silk were still required to maintain a monopoly of the technical skills used in silk's manufacture and to ensure that silk was sold only to those entitled by the government to wear it. Since purple dye and silk textiles dyed purple were strictly an imperial monopoly, the dyers in Constantinople faced harsh punishments if they used purple dye for commercial purposes. The perfumers in Constantinople dealt with many dyes, aromatic spices, and fragrant resins that were essential for the Christian religious liturgy, and they, too, had to follow the sumptuary rules when trading in these commodities. The following regulations indicate how thoroughly the Byzantine state controlled its commerce and its people. How important was the silk monopoly for the Byzantine regime?*

"Roman Law in the Later Roman Empire," in *The Book of the Eparch* (ca. 895), trans. E. H. Field (Cambridge, U,K,, 1938; reprint, London: Variorum Reprints, 1970), 236–37, 239–40, 241–43, 245–47, 249–51.

Merchants of Silk Stuffs

1. The silk merchants will be concerned in the purchase of silk garments. They will not engage in other purchases except those articles they require for their personal use, and they are forbidden to sell the latter. They are moreover forbidden to resell to persons who are "strangers" to the city the articles which are on the prohibited list, that is to say purple of the distinctive dyes (red or ? violet), so as to prevent exportation of these out of the Empire. Offenders will be flogged and liable to confiscation.

2. Silk merchants whether freemen or slaves who purchase from the nobility or silk buyers, or from anyone else, garments exceeding ten *nomismata*[1] in value shall declare the same to the eparch so that he may know where these articles are to be sold. Offenders will suffer the above-named punishments.

3. Anyone else who has not declared to the eparch the peach-coloured or red garments or mantles of two-thirds dye will be punished.

4. Any person who fails to inform the eparch of a sale of an article destined for aliens of the Empire, so that the eparch may certify the transaction, shall be held responsible.

5. To obtain admittance to the guild of silk merchants five members of the craft must testify to the eparch that the candidate is a person worthy to exercise the craft. He shall then be admitted to it, he shall open a shop, and carry on business. His entrance fee to the guild is six *nomismata*.

6. To obtain a licence to acquire the workshop of a silk merchant the tax is ten *nomismata*. The recommendation of the eparch is necessary.

7. Every person exercising at one and the same time the craft of silk merchant and silk dyer shall be put to his election to choose one or other of these crafts to the exclusion of the other. Anyone attempting to carry on both crafts shall be liable to the aforesaid punishments.

8. Care must be taken to ensure that strangers who lodge in caravanserais do not purchase prohibited or unsewn garments, unless for their personal use; and in the latter case the articles must have been manufactured in Constantinople.

When strangers leave the city their departure must be notified to the eparch so that he may take cognizance of the articles they have purchased.

---

[1] A gold coin of about sixty-eight grams.

Anyone helping them to evade this obligation shall be flogged, shaved and have his property confiscated.

9. Every silk merchant who secretly or openly causes the rent of any other silk merchant to be raised, shall be flogged, shaved and shall be liable to confiscation.

Merchants of Manufactured Goods Imported from Syria and Bagdad

1. These merchants shall obey a single "exarch" nominated by the eparch. They are forbidden to deal in any other trade reserved to the silk merchants, or to purchase any kind of manufactured goods, other than those of Syrian origin, and silk goods imported from Seleucia or other similar locality.

Let those who contravene these rules be flogged, shaved and expelled from the guild.

2. Imports destined for *prandiopratai*[2] must be deposited in bulk in a warehouse where the members of the craft shall meet and share them. The same procedure shall be observed for the following articles termed saracen derived from Syria, under garments, cloaks of ribbed wool, shot or watered silk dresses, garments with sleeves of single or double texture, and manufactures of Bagdad. All those merchants shall have the privilege of purchasing these articles. They shall share them with Syrian merchants who have been domiciled in this city for at least ten years.

The place of sale shall be in the same quarter of the *Embolê* [arcades of the bazaar] instead of in undetermined localities. Anyone refusing to conform to this rule shall suffer the above-named penalties.

3. Upon the arrival of the goods let all the members of the guild contribute to a fund, each according to his means, for the purchase thereof, and they shall then be shared out to the members under the direction of the eparch according to their respective contributions.

4. Whatever may be the importance of a consignment of Syrian goods arriving in the capital, the guild of *prandiopratai* shall buy all the goods of superior or inferior qualities comprised in the consignment. Should they be dye stuffs or perfumes those articles shall be purchased by the dyers or perfumers.

If, apart from those guilds, a nobleman or a general residing in the city desires to acquire a part of the consignment directly from the

[2] The guild for merchants of manufactured goods.

consignors he shall be allowed to do so to the extent of his consumption for his personal requirements in his own household.

5. Syrians who have come to Constantinople with merchandize are not permitted to stay in Constantinople for more than three months in the caravanserais. During those three months they must complete their sales and effect their purchases. All the foreign articles which their customers may have entrusted to them for sale on account shall be declared by them to the exarch, and he shall dispose of them to the best advantage.

All persons who do not conform to these rules shall be flogged, shaved, and have their property confiscated.

Raw Silk Merchants

1. Merchants in this class are limited to exercising their own trade, and must do so publicly in the public places which are assigned to them. Anyone contravening this shall be flogged, shaved and banished.

2. Every raw silk merchant who employs a workman for wages must only engage him for one month. He shall not advance him more than a month's salary, that is to say the amount he can earn in thirty days, and whoever pays in excess of that sum shall forfeit the excess.

3. A raw silk merchant is forbidden to engage an employee of another member of his craft until such employee has worked for the latter for the full period for which he was engaged. Any contravention is to be punished by the forfeit of that part of the salary which the employee has received without having worked for it.

4. For each cantar of raw silk the raw silk merchant shall pay to the exarchs (of the guild) one *keration*.[3] All those craftsmen whose scales or weights do not bear the sealed impress of the eparch shall be flogged and shaved.

5. Individuals who have come to lodge with raw silk in the caravanserais have no fee to pay for selling it. They shall only pay their rent and for the right of sojourn. Nor shall those who buy raw silk be required to pay any fee.

6. To secure admission to the guild the testimony of honourable and honest men must be produced by the candidate, testifying to his good repute. Admission can then be granted on payment to the guild of ten *nomismata*.

---

[3] A silver coin of about thirty-two grams.

7. If a raw silk merchant wishes to entrust his business to one of his slaves the latter will hold his master's guarantee, and will be, like his master, liable for any dishonest acts committed by him.

8. At the opening of the market all the members of the guild shall contribute according to their means to a fund to purchase the raw silk which shall then be rationed among them in proportion to their respective contributions.

9. If a rich raw silk merchant wishes to sell to one of his poorer brethren raw silk acquired from some importer, the profit he may secure shall not exceed one *keration* per *nomisma*.

10. Every raw silk merchant who does not have a fixed salary but imports raw silk in his own name for some rich or influential person or for a silk dyer, shall be flogged and shaved, and cease to be a member of the guild.

11. Anyone who by means of a trick tries to raise the price of raw silk after having received from the purchaser earnest money for the same, shall be condemned to forfeit it.

12. Every raw silk merchant convicted of having travelled outside the city to buy raw silk shall cease to be a member of the guild.

13. Raw silk merchants shall sell their wares in the public streets and not in their private premises, lest such sales be made to persons who are not authorized to buy. Anyone contravening shall be flogged and shaved.

14. The raw silk merchants shall not be permitted to dress silk but only to trade in it. Persons contravening shall be liable to the aforesaid punishments.

15. The folk called [dyers?] shall not trade in pure silk either secretly or openly, and those who disobey shall be liable to the aforesaid punishments.

16. Raw silk merchants are forbidden to sell raw silk to Jews or to tradesfolk who would resell it outside the city. Persons contravening will be flogged and shaved.

Silk Dyers

1. Dyers are forbidden to make up the purple of the so-called prohibited grades, that is to say in the series of great mantles, including those of self colour or those where the purple alternates with dark green or yellow in half-tint. They may dye peach tint where that colour is combined with others, or common turbans of slavonian style slashed with scarlet bands. Peach-coloured purple and fine dresses of [?] "two palms"

length must be declared to the eparch and also the cloaks worth more than ten *nomismata*, even if of divers colours.

2. All noblemen and simple citizens are forbidden to make cloaks of purple of six or eight lyes. This prohibition does not extend to cloaks of ten or twelve lyes provided the tints are real purple and are of small type and such as would not come within the category of dyed material which the eparch must reserve for the use of the imperial house of the sovereign. And this includes the cloaks rounded at the lower part reserved for the prince's use, excepting those of shorter model which fall in folds on the tunic, counting at least ten lyes and coloured in different tints.

Whoever is convicted of making articles which we forbid shall be liable to have his goods confiscated and shall cease trading.

3. Whoever refuses to open his premises for inspection by the inspector of seals or the inspector of cloths, or who sells to aliens to the city a cloak worth more than ten *nomismata* shall be flogged and shaved.

4. Whoever dyes raw silk with blood (i.e. synon. with the liquid of murex) or converts it into parti-coloured purple, double, triple or two-thirds red, shall have his hand cut off.

5. Whoever sells goods to aliens without the knowledge of the eparch shall have his goods confiscated.

6. Whoever attempts to carry on at one and the same time the trade of *sericarius*[4] and *vestiopratis*[5] shall be put on his election to choose one trade or the other.

7. Every dyer who sells a slave, a workman, or a foreman craftsman, to persons alien to the city or the Empire, shall have his hand cut off.

8. Dyers shall buy raw silk from the raw silk merchant. If they buy it from aliens of the city they shall be flogged, shaved and cease trading.

9. Should bales of cloaks be found in the store-shops of the dyers which do not bear the eparch's stamp the same shall be confiscated and the workman who had them shall have his goods confiscated.

10. If a dyer receives the workman of another dyer wittingly before such workman has finished the work for which he was paid he shall be fined an amount equal to what the workman had not earned by his work.

11. Anyone who has purchased garments made outside the city and delivers them to the imperial store shall be flogged and shaved. . . .

13. Anyone wishing to open a workshop must, if he is a freeman, be guaranteed by five persons. If he is a slave his master must be surety for

---

[4] The silk dyers' guild.
[5] The guild for merchants of finished silk textiles that are ready to be made into garments.

him; providing him also with adequate means. In both cases the guarantors will be subject to the same liabilities as the person for whom they stand surety. And he shall pay an entrance fee of three *nomismata*.

Perfumers

1. Let every perfumer have his own place and not attempt to cheat his competitor.

Let the members of the guild by watching over one another prevent the retailing of debased wares. They shall keep no inferior spices or wares in their shops. A sweet smell has nothing in common with a nasty smell.

Let them sell

> pepper
> spikenard
> cinnamon
> aloes wood
> amber
> musk
> incense
> myrrh
> balsam
> indigo
> sweet-smelling herbs
> mint[?]
> thapsia, wood for yellow dye
> caper

in short any article which is used for perfumery or for dyeing.

Let their counters stand in a line comprised between the *miliarion* and the revered eikon of Christ, our divine Lord, which stands above the bronze portico, so that the sweet perfume may waft upwards to the eikon and at the same time permeate the vestibule of the imperial palace.

Anyone contravening these rules shall be flogged, shaved and banished.

2. When the above-mentioned articles come from the land of the Chaldees, Trebizond, or any other place, the perfumers shall buy them from the importers on the days appointed by the regulations.

It is forbidden to hoard these commodities so as to sell them at a period of dearth, or to exact an undue profit above what is fair when they are scarce, or enhance the price unduly. Importers shall not reside in the capital for more than three months. They are to sell their goods expeditiously and then return home.

Anyone contravening these rules shall be liable to the aforesaid penalties.

3. Any perfumer who secretly or openly tries to raise the rent of a colleague shall be flogged, shaved and expelled from the guild.

4. Any perfumer who is convicted of having filed or sweated *nomismata*, or of having refused to take a *tetarteron* bearing the effigy of the Emperor for authenticity, or of having hoarded coins, instead of sending them to his bankers, whose function he would thus usurp, shall be liable to the aforesaid penalties.

5. Every perfumer and generally speaking every artisan convicted of dishonestly raising the price of wares when the price has already been fixed with the purchaser and the latter has paid earnest money on the deal, shall be liable to a fine equivalent to the deposit made by the purchaser.

No member of the guild is allowed to purchase wares which come within the purview of the grocers' trade or are sold by steelyard.

Perfumers shall only buy articles which are sold by weight on scales. Anyone contravening these rules shall suffer the aforesaid penalties.

6. If a perfumer carries on the trade of a grocer, he shall be given an option of selecting one or the other of these trades. And he shall be forbidden to carry on the trade which he does not choose to follow.

6

The Tang Empire and Foreign Traders and Priests, Eighth–Tenth Centuries

22

ZHANG ZHUO

Anecdotes from the Court and the Country

ca. 705

Zhang Zhuo (ca. 660–740) was a famous writer whose book of anecdotes about the Tang court and society focuses on the time when Empress Wu Zetian (r. 684–704) declared her sovereignty. Though Zhang Zhuo was critical of the empress, the events he describes show that her reign was a time of prosperity, with many foreign traders settling in the cities of Tang China. His anecdotes illuminate aspects of daily life among the merchant and professional classes. They indicate, for example, that the Chinese did not always understand foreign religious rituals or distinguish among the different religions practiced by foreigners. They also expose robbers and imposters who sought to profit from Silk Roads trade, and they reveal the nature of ambition and patronage in Tang China, especially the desire to wear the robe of purple silk that conferred status. How did foreign traders practice their religion in Tang China? How did they survive and prosper in Chinese society at that time?

Zhang Zhuo, *Chaoye Jianzai* [Anecdotes from the Court and the Country] (Beijing: Zhonghua Shuju, 1979), 64–65, 75, 114, 148. Translated by Xinru Liu.

[Sogdian Rituals]

In Henan Fu[1] Zoroastrian temples were built in the vicinity of South Market, in the neighborhoods known as Lide Fang and Xi Fang. Each year foreign traders[2] celebrate their holidays in these temples. They cook pigs and sheep; play music on the *pipa*,[3] the drum, and the flute; and sing and dance as if they are intoxicated. After sprinkling wine to worship their god, they hire a Hu[4] man to be the master of the ritual, and all the spectators donate money to him. The master takes a knife, which is as bright as frost and is so sharp that a hair blown against it would be cut through, and then sticks it in his own belly until its tip emerges on his back. He then uses the knife to churn his belly, causing his stomach and intestines to bleed. After about one mealtime,[5] he sprays water on the wound and chants some incantations. Then the belly recovers as if nothing happened. This is just a magic trick performed in the Western Regions.[6]

In Liangzhou,[7] there are Zoroastrian temples. On the day the god is worshipped, the ritual master hammers a long iron nail into his head until it extends all the way to his armpit. Once he walks out of the gate, his movement is as light as if he were flying, and he covers several hundred *li*[8] in a moment. When he arrives at a Zoroastrian temple in the Western Region, he dances to the rhythmic beat of a song. Then he returns to the temple in Liangzhou to take out the nail, and there is no trace of any wound on his body. Afterward he lies down for about ten days and recovers totally. No one understands how this trick is performed. . . .

[A Robber of Travelers]

He Mingyuan of Dingzhou[9] is extremely rich. He is in charge of three official post stations and has also opened hotels alongside the post stations that provide boarding for traders, all the better to rob Hu traders of their goods. He thus accumulated tons of wealth and established a

---

[1] Another name for the city of Luoyang, the second capital of the Tang Empire.
[2] The foreign traders in this context are mostly Sogdians.
[3] A plucked string instrument with a fretted fingerboard.
[4] A foreigner; in this context, a Sogdian.
[5] A way to count time, about twenty minutes.
[6] In this context, Sogdiana.
[7] Now in Gansu Province.
[8] During the Tang dynasty, one *li* was about one-third of a mile.
[9] Now in Hebei Province.

factory with five hundred looms weaving damask silk. However, there came a time when he felt that he was too old to engage in such violence and thus stopped robbing travelers. His household was immediately bankrupted. Then he resumed the business of robbery and recovered all his wealth. . . .

[A Foreign Imposter]

During the Zhou era,[10] a Brahman named Huifan was as cunning and seductive as a fox. He often used witchcraft to cause disasters, and he fussed around royalty like a mouse in order to gain favors and power by devious means. The Empress Wu Zetian treated him as if he were a saintly priest and gave him numerous gifts. The Princess Taiping thought that he was an Indian king and thus treated him as royalty. He became very influential and glorified. During the reign of Xiaohe [?], he often rode on official horses when entering the royal palaces. During the coronation ceremonies, he was the one who ran errands in and out of the Forbidden City[11] gates. Every time he was in the audience of the sovereign, plenty of silk damask and gauze as well as gold and silver vessels were granted to him. He was arrogant and condescending, since most of the royal treasures had become his property. He often interpreted omens and predicted good fortunes as well as disasters without real divine vision. During the Shenwu era,[12] Huifan was executed. The entire capital city applauded the event. . . .

[Wang Xian, Who Died for a Purple Robe]

Wang Xian had been an acquaintance of the Emperor Wenwu[13] since they were very young, ever since an incident that involved Yan Ziling [?]. They often played together, dragging each other by the pants and grabbing each other's hats for fun. The emperor, before he came to the throne, frequently teased him: "Wang Xian won't be able to make a cocoon for himself until he is old."[14] Soon after the emperor ascended the throne, Wang Xian requested an audience to see him,

---

[10] The reign of Empress Wu Zetian (684–704).

[11] A residential courtyard for the royal family and for those who held the highest offices, reporting directly to the emperor. No outsiders were allowed.

[12] The Shenwu era is probably the Shenlong era (705–707), at the beginning of the reign of Li Xian, the successor to Wu Zetian.

[13] Taizon (r. 627–649).

[14] Meaning that he could never mature.

and then asked him, "Is your subject now able to make a cocoon?" The emperor answered him with a smile: "This is not yet sure." The emperor summoned his three sons and granted all of them a fifth rank official position. Wang Xian was the only one left out. The emperor told him: "It is not that I do not want to give you the favor. You do not look like a person serving in a high position."[15] Wang Xian replied: "If I can receive a noble status in the morning, I would not mind dying that same night." At that time, Fang Xuanling, the prime minister, advised the emperor saying: "As your Majesty has enjoyed a friendship with him since your youth, why not just try granting him a position to see how it works?" The emperor thus granted him a position of the third rank, with the purple robe and golden belt. Wang Xian died that same night.

[15] Meaning that a high position might hurt him.

23

JINGJING

Inscriptions from the Nestorian Stele

781

In the early seventeenth century, near the Tang dynasty's capital city of Chang'an, Christian missionaries discovered a stone stele inscribed in both Chinese and Syriac, an ancient language used by eastern Christian churches. Using both Buddhist and Daoist terminology, these inscriptions, dated 781, explain the doctrines of Christianity, its arrival and flourishing in China, and the patronage its priests received, including having purple robes bestowed upon them by Tang emperors and ministers. Many members of the congregation signed the bottom part of the stone stele, using both Chinese and Syriac scripts; the Christian monk who composed the text was named Jingjing. The following passage describes the Christian faith and the development of the Christian church in China. Even

Zhongxi Jiaotong Shiliao Huibian [Historical Documents on the Communications between China and the West], ed. Zhang Xinglang, rev. Zhu Xueqin (Beijing: Zhonghua Shuju, 2003), 1:215–29. Translated by Xinru Liu.

*though these missionaries were Nestorian Christians, a sect condemned
as heretical by the Byzantine ecclesiastical hierarchy as early as 431,
Jingjing tries to connect Nestorian Christianity with the long-gone glory
days of the Roman Empire. Where did the Nestorian Christian missionaries come from in the Silk Road system?*

[The Messiah of Christians]

Thus one of the Trinity, the Messiah of Christians, concealing his true
divinity, came to the world as a man. Angels declared his coming, and
the Virgin gave birth to the Holy One in Da Qin.[1] Seeing the splendor
of a bright star indicating this auspicious moment, the Persians brought
their tribute to the Holy One.

Having fulfilled the traditional laws set by twenty-four earlier saints,
He made a great plan for families and states. He set up a new doctrine of
the pure and silent spirit of the Trinity, using the right faith to cultivate
morality. . . .

[The Development of the Christian Church in China]

In the country of Da Qin there was a great priest whose name was Rabban. He carried the true scriptures and suffered extreme hardship to
make his way to [China], and he reached the city of Chang'an in the
ninth year of the Zhenguan era.[2] His Majesty, the Emperor, appointed
the prime minister, Fang Xuanling, to be the head of a ceremonial group
that went out to a western suburb of the capital city where they could
welcome him and accompany him to the royal palace. In the imperial
library Rabban translated the sacred scripture, and he discussed the
doctrine of religion in the Forbidden Royal Residence.[3] The Emperor
came to a deep understanding of the true teachings of Christianity and
gave an order that it should be taught within his realm. He issued an
edict in the seventh month, in the autumn, of the twelfth year of the Zhenguan era saying: "There can be more than one name for the Way along
which the sacred path runs; there can also be different ways to express
sacredness. Religions take different forms at different places to help a
large population. The Archbishop Rabban traveled a great distance from

---

[1] Da Qin is the traditional name that Chinese historians gave to the Roman Empire
and later the Byzantine Empire.

[2] 645.

[3] The residential enclosure for the emperor's immediate family.

the Da Qin country in order to present the scripture and images of the saints to my court. After learning from its doctrine, I feel the religion is beautiful, mystic and peaceful. Its basic doctrine provides the essential teachings and there are no redundant words and all are pure truth. It is helpful to all the people and therefore should be spread to all the lands under the heaven." Thus the government built the Da Qin Monastery in the Yiningfang ward of the capital, and ordered twenty-one monks to be ordained staying there. . . .

According to *Pictures and Maps of the Western Region*[4] and historical documents dated to the Han and Wei dynasties, the country of Da Qin controls the Coral Sea to its south; on its north side it is located next to the Treasure Mountains; looking toward the west there is a fairyland of flowers and woods; and on its eastern side it is next to the place where winds blow year round and the Ruoshui River flows. The land produces a cloth that can be washed with fire,[5] incense that can restore souls, pearls as bright as the moon, and jade that shines in the dark.[6] There are neither thieves nor robbers. People are happy and healthy. Christianity is the only religion and the only law, and only highly moral men become rulers. Great cultural and material prosperity spread to the vast land.

Emperor Gaozong[7] followed his ancestor's path by supporting the true religion. He had Christian churches established in each prefecture and appointed Rabban as the Great Lord of Law Stabilizing the Country. Christian law spread throughout the land, and the country prospered tremendously. As a hundred cities had Christian churches, the people's homes were rich, and the church became affluent. However, during the Shengli era,[8] the Buddhists were influential, and they slandered Christians in front of the Empress Wu. At the end of the Xiantian era,[9] some Daoists made fun of Christianity and slandered the religion in Xihao.[10] A great head priest Abraham and Archbishop Gabriel, along with many noble people from the golden region [?] and honorable

---

[4] This is likely a book about geography circulating at the time and no longer extant.
[5] Asbestos.
[6] This geographic description is vague. It appears to describe Italy, then it jumps to what seems to be the Takla Makan region, where the wind is strong and the rivers are seasonal. *Ruoshui* literally means "weak river." The Tien Shan Mountains north of the Takla Makan Desert are famous for their jade. The regions between these two areas, famous for incense and pearls, go unnamed.
[7] Gaozong (r. 650–683).
[8] 698–700.
[9] 712–713, in the reign of Emperor Xuanzong.
[10] Another name for Chang'an, the capital of the Tang Empire.

priests who had given up worldly interests, reorganized the networks of Christians. Emperor Xuanzong ordered five princes, headed by Ningguo, to visit the blessed church in order to rebuild the sacred altar. After the destruction, the columns of law became even taller, and the once tilted sacred foundation was made flat again. In the early Tianbao era[11] the emperor ordered the great general Gao Lishi to set the portraits of five saints in the church, with a grant of one hundred rolls of silk. . . .

In the third year [of the Tianbao era], a monk named George following the direction of stars came to the direction of the sun in order to pay homage to the Emperor. The Emperor summoned monk Abraham, Pulun [Paul?], and all together seventeen people to join Archbishop George to perform rituals in the Xingqing Palace in order to increase the religious merits that the Emperor could claim. That was when the Emperor, his Majesty, wrote the name of the church on a plate that was placed on the church gate. . . .

The great patron of the church is Isaac, *Guanglu Dafu* in a Gold and Purple Robe,[12] the lieutenant governor of the Northern Frontier and superintendent of the Royal Examination Palace as well as a priest who received a purple cleric robe. He is kind and generous, and he attends Christian worship services and follows their teachings. He is highly skilled in many different fields. His knowledge is quite versatile, and he is from Rajagraha.[13]

[11] 742–756.

[12] The *Guanglu Dafu* is the highest ranking official title; thus the officer is entitled to wear the gold and purple robe.

[13] This Rajagraha is not the famous city in eastern India where Buddha often preached, but the city of Balkh in Afghanistan. After the Kushan period, it became the home of a strong Buddhist establishment and thus an important center of Buddhist learning. After the Abbasid Caliphate conquered the city, Isaac decided to leave Rajagraha to seek his fortune in China.

24

LIU XU AND OTHERS

The Old Tang History

941–945

*Liu Xu was a chief minister under the Later Jin dynasty (936–946), one of
the short-lived regimes that followed the demise of the Tang dynasty in 907.
He inherited the job of compiling an official history of the Tang dynasty
from his predecessors at court, and eventually he signed the book that he
worked on with others. Work on the history began soon after the dynasty's
end. Not only were many archives available, but some people from Tang
times were still alive to provide information. The history proved to be a
thorough record of the Tang dynasty, which lasted almost three hundred
years. The structure of the narrative is not always logical, as the work
was done in a hurry. Nevertheless, the conflict between the Tang emperor
Wuzong (r. 841–847) and the Buddhist establishment, as well as other
foreign religions, is recorded as a series of chronological decrees. What were
the emperor's objections to religious establishments? How did the changes
in the economic and political conditions of Silk Roads trading partners
affect not only commerce but also religious attitudes?*

On the *gengzi* day in the seventh month of autumn,[1] the emperor
[Wuzong] issued an edict to restrict the numbers of Buddhist monasteries under heaven.[2] The Secretariat Chancellery submitted a memorial
to the throne:

> According to the rules and statutes of the law, officers of superior
> prefectures should perform the ceremony of burning incense in
> temples on anniversaries of ancestor emperors. Therefore, may Your
> Majesty allow one monastery in every superior prefecture wherein all

[1] August 31, 845.
[2] That is, in the empire.

Jiu Tangshu [The Old Tang History], in *Hawai'i Reader in Traditional Chinese Culture*,
ed. Victor Mair, Nancy Steinhardt, and Paul Goldin (Honolulu: University of Hawai'i
Press, 2005), 377–79. Translated by Xinru Liu and Victor Mair, with minor changes to
suit the format of this Bedford series book.

the statues of sacred figures could be sheltered; monasteries in inferior prefectures should be closed. Please allow ten monasteries on the two major streets of both Chang'an and Luoyang to stay, with ten monks allowed to remain in each monastery.

His Majesty issued an imperial order which said:

It is fitting that monasteries be allowed to remain in superior prefectures, but only those of fine workmanship may stay. Those that are dilapidated, though located in superior prefectures, should also be closed and torn down. On anniversaries when incense is to be burned, it is appropriate for officials to carry out the rituals at Taoist temples. Two monasteries are allowed to stay on each of the [two main] streets in both the Upper Capital [Chang'an] and the Lower Capital [Luoyang], and thirty monks are allowed to remain in each monastery. On the Left Street of the Upper Capital, Ci'en Monastery and Jianfu Monastery may stay. On the Right Street, Ximing Monastery and Zhuangyan Monastery may stay.

The Secretariat submitted another memorial to the throne:

As most of the monasteries under heaven are to be closed, bronze statues, bells, and gongs should be handed over to the Salt and Iron Monopoly Commissioner to be cast into coins; iron statues should be handed over to prefectures where the monasteries are located and cast into agricultural tools. Gold, silver, and brass statues and statues of other materials should be melted down for government expenditure. All the gold, silver, bronze, and iron statues in the homes of nobles and commoners must be turned over to the government offices within one month after this edict is issued. Those who do not obey this order should be punished by the Ministry of the Salt and Iron Monopoly Commissioner according to the "Law of Banning Possession of Bronze." Statues made of clay, wood, and stone are allowed to remain in the monasteries as before.

The Secretariat again submitted a memorial to the throne:

Monks and nuns should not be administered by the Ministry of Sacrifices. They should be administered by the Court of State Ceremonial. As Buddhist monasteries are banned, other heterodox religions such as the Roman church[3] and Zoroastrian shrines should not be allowed either. Staff of these religious institutions should be ordered to return to secular life and to their home places as taxpayers. The foreigners of those religious institutions should be returned to their proper places to be administered.

---

[3] The Nestorian Christian church.

In the eighth month, a decree was issued:

I, the sovereign, have heard that, in the Three Dynasties[4] period of antiquity, there was no mention of Buddhism. Only after the Han and the Wei dynasties did the doctrine of images[5] gradually arise. Thus, the propagation of this strange custom started in that late time and, in accord with the circumstances, has tainted our practices, spreading and multiplying. It has developed to the extent that, though it eats away at our national customs, we no longer notice; it seduces people and makes them confused. It has penetrated to mountains and plains all over the empire and within the city walls of the two capitals. The number of monks daily increases, and monasteries are growing in grandeur. Buddhist construction projects cost much human labor, while monastic ornaments of gold and other treasures deprive society of much benefit. Religious teachers have come to replace rulers and fathers; monastic discipline separates husband and wife. No other religion is more harmful to the law and human relations than Buddhism. Furthermore, when one farmer is not cultivating the land, there must be someone starving as a result; when one woman is not raising silkworms, there must be someone shivering in the cold.

At the present moment, there are innumerable monks and nuns under heaven who wait for farmers to feed them and women to clothe them. Temples and monasteries have been constructed extravagantly tall and ostentatiously ornamented, defying regulations and daring to imitate the style of royal palaces. During the Jin, Song, Qi, and Liang dynasties,[6] these practices caused the depletion of material wealth and labor and the deterioration of moral standards. Moreover, my ancestors Gaozu and Taizong pacified turmoil through military force and administered China with a civil system. These two instruments are quite sufficient for running the country. How can this trivial religion from the west contend with our state structure! During the eras of Zhenguan and Kaiyuan,[7] there were also efforts to eliminate Buddhism. However, the eradication was not thorough, thus its influence became even greater. I, the sovereign, after broadly surveying what has been discussed in previous times and seeking out current opinion, realize that whether this corrupt practice can be eliminated depends on determination. Meanwhile, all the loyal officers inside or outside the court who assist me wholeheartedly have submitted appropriate recommendations to

---

[4] The Three Dynasties are the earliest—Xia, Shang, and Zhou—in Chinese chronicles.

[5] "Doctrine of images" is a technical term referring to the second stage in the development of Buddhism, but here it is used loosely to signify Buddhism in general. [Translators' note.]

[6] Dynasties that ruled southern China from 317 to 556.

[7] Eras from 627 to 742.

me, saying that the reform should be enforced. Why should I avoid this action, which will block the origin of evil that has prevailed for a thousand years, protect the integrity of the royal code enacted by a hundred kings, and benefit all the people?

When the 4,600 and more major monasteries under heaven are demolished, 260,500 monks and nuns will return to secular life to become taxpayers in the Double Tax system;[8] when more than 40,000 small monasteries and temples are demolished, several million hectares of fertile land will be confiscated, and 150,000 male and female slaves will become taxpayers in the Double Tax system. The remaining monks and nuns are to be placed under the supervision of the Bureau of Receptions [for Foreign Guests]; thus the fact that Buddhism is a religion for foreigners will be made obvious. The 3,000 and more followers of Christianity and Zoroastrianism are ordered to return to secular life to maintain the purity of Chinese mores.

Oh! It seems as though that which has not been carried out in the past is about to become true! How can one claim that those institutions will never be eliminated when they are completely gone? More than 100,000 idle and lazy persons have already been driven out of monasteries; thousands and thousands of those useless, colorful houses have been demolished. From now on, our motto is to be quiet and pure, and our model is to follow the principle of nonaction. Our administration should be simple and efficient, following only one style. All the people of the country should be subjects of the empire. As this is the beginning of the reform, there is no known omen, so I have issued this edict clarifying matters to the court in order to make you understand my intention. . . .

On *jiachen* day in the eleventh month,[9] the emperor issued an edict:

Because monks and nuns have returned to secular life, no one is in charge of the lands for charity and houses for sick people. I am afraid the crippled and the sick will have no food supply. The two capitals should provide monasteries with a suitable amount of charity lands. Every prefecture and superior prefecture should set aside [approximately] seventeen to twenty-five acres and select an elder local to manage them, in order to make grain available for porridge [for the poor.]

[8] The "Double Tax" was a taxation system established around 780 CE. In this new system, taxes were calculated according to the number of laborers and the amount of property owned by the tax-paying household, not purely on the number of households as in the previous system. Taxes were collected twice a year, after the harvests of the summer and autumn; thus it was called "Double Tax." [Translators' note.]

[9] December 3, 845.

7

Muslim Baghdad in the Eurasian Market, Ninth–Eleventh Centuries

25

SULAYMAN AL-TAJIR AND OTHERS

An Account of China and India

ca. 851

In the ninth-century Indian Ocean trading world, Siraf, a port on the Persian Gulf, was one place where sailors and traders gathered around a lamp in an inn and told stories about what they had seen or heard on their journeys. Sometime around 851, Sulayman al-Tajir, whose cousin was the governor of Siraf, and some of his fellow Arab merchants compiled an account about China and India. Their stories, like all those collected by sailors and merchants, represented firsthand information as well as fantasies heard from others. Whatever the truth of their stories, they noticed that the Chinese ate many of the same fruits and vegetables that people in their own homeland enjoyed. They were much impressed by the abundance of silk clothing in China and by the Chinese beverage tea. They reported the way Chinese produced porcelain—yet to become China's top export. The traders did not object to government regulations and tariffs. They were law-abiding foreigners who applied for and obtained travel documents and trading permits, just as their predecessors had done centuries before during the Han dynasty. How accurate was the commercial information obtained by the Arab maritime traders?

Sulaymān al-Tājir and Others, *An Account of China and India*, in *Arabic Classical Accounts of India and China*, trans. S. Maqbul Ahmad (Shimla: Indian Institute of Advanced Study, 1989), 41–42, 46, 49–50.

The dress of the people of China, young and old, consists of silk during winter as well as summer. As for the kings they wear fine silk. Those below them [wear] what they can afford. In winter, they wear two, three, four, five and even more trousers according to what they can afford. Their objects [*sic*] is to keep the lower parts [of their body] warm due to intense cold which they fear. But in summer they wear a single silk shirt or something like that. They do not wear turbans.

Their food consists of rice, and sometimes they cook stew, which they pour over the rice and then eat it. The members of royal houses eat wheat bread and meat of all the animals and pork and [meat] of other [animals]. Among the fruits they have apple, peach, citron, pomegranate, quince, pear, banana, sugar-cane, melon, fig, grape, cucumber, glossy cucumber, crab-apple, walnut, almond, hazel-nut, pistachio, plum, apricot, sorb and coconut. They do not have in their country many date-palms except a [solitary] date-palm tree in the house of one of them. Their drink consists of the intoxicating drink prepared from rice. They do not have wine in their country, nor is it exported to them. They neither know about it, nor do they drink it. It is from rice that vinegar, the intoxicating wine, sweet-meat and things resembling them are prepared. . . .

They [the Chinese] conduct their transactions in cowries,[1] and their treasures are similar to those of the other kings. None of the kings except these has cowries which form the special currency of the land. They also have gold, silver, pearls, brocade and silk: all these they possess in abundance except that these form their property while the cowries are the currency. Their imports consist of ivory, incense, [and] ingots of copper. . . . They possess numerous beasts of burden; they do not have the Arabian horse but other [breeds]; they have donkeys and the two-humped camels in plenty. They have excellent cohesive green clay out of which they manufacture goblets as thin as the flasks, through which the sparkle of the water can be seen. . . . When the sailors enter [China] from the sea, the Chinese hold their goods and store them in godowns,[2] and leave them under the custody of police for six months till the next batch of sailors come in. Then, 3/10th of the goods is taken [as duty] and remaining part is restored to the merchants. Then, whatever the government wishes to take, [it] buys at the highest price and pays the amount immediately, and in this transaction they do not act unjustly. . . .

Among the important sources of revenue of the king are salt and an herb which they mix in hot water and then drink. It [the hot drink]

---

[1] Small copper coins issued by the Chinese government.
[2] Warehouses.

is sold in every town at a very high price. . . . It is more leafy than the green trefoil and slightly more perfumed, and has a soury taste. [For preparing it] they boil water and then sprinkle the leaves over it. It is a cure for them for everything. All that goes into the treasury consists of the poll-tax, salt and this herb. . . .

Anyone intending to travel from one place to the other has to have two documents: one from the king and the other from the eunuch. The royal document is meant for the journey and has the name of the person, names of the persons accompanying him, his age, age of his companion, and the name of his tribe [entered] in it. It is incumbent upon everyone living in China whether they be its inhabitants, Arabs or anyone else to trace back their origin to something for identification. As for the document issued by the eunuch, it contains a description of the money and the merchandise carried by the traveller. This is because along their route there are armed guards who examine the two documents. So, when anyone reaches them, they write: "So and so son of so and so, belonging to such and such [a tribe], reached us on such and such a day, such and such a month, and such and such a year, and he had such and such things with him." This is done so that the money or the merchandise of the person does not get lost; if it does or if the person dies, it becomes known how it is lost and it is returned to him or to his descendants after him.

26

MAS'UDI

The Meadows of Gold: The Abbasids

ca. 947

Mas'udi (896–956) was born in Baghdad, the capital of Abbasid Caliphate, and died in Egypt. He wrote about his extensive travels in the Islamic world, the Byzantine Empire, and India, and his early years in Baghdad also enabled him to write a candid history of Abbasid court life. The

Mas'udi, *The Meadows of Gold: The Abbasids*, trans. and ed. Paul Lunde and Caroline Stone (London: Kegan Paul, 1989), 228–29.

following account records how Mu'tasim, a younger son of Harun al-Rashid (r. 786–809), started to recruit Turkish slaves from Central Asia to strengthen his power even before he became caliph in 833. These Turks came from a steppe background where nomadic horsemen flourished, and they were loyal and well-trained soldiers. Hoping this alien military force could be imposed on the various peoples within the well-established Islamic empire, Mu'tasim treated them well and dressed them in bright silk brocade to distinguish them from the regular army. What does this account reveal about imperial expansion?

Mu'tasim sought out Turks and had them bought by his freedmen. He thus gathered together a troop of 4,000, whom he dressed in brocade with gilded belts and ornaments, distinguishing them by their costume from the rest of the army. He also formed for his service a corps made up of soldiers from the two districts of Egypt, the district of Yemen and that of Qais, and he called them the Maghribis—"Westerners." He also fitted out men from Khurasan and in particular Fergana and Ushrusana. These Turks soon made up a numerous army. They subjected the inhabitants of Baghdad to great annoyance, riding their horses at full gallop through the middle of the markets and doing much harm to the infirm and to children. On several occasions the people took vengeance and killed more than one horseman who had knocked over a woman, an old man, a child or someone blind.

Mu'tasim therefore decided to move the Turks away from his capital and to settle them on a great plain. He encamped first at Baradan, four parasangs from Baghdad, but finding this place neither sufficiently healthy, nor yet sufficiently large, he continued to move about, exploring different areas along the Tigris and elsewhere. In this way, he came to a place named Qatul, the climate of which pleased him. There was a village there inhabited by the Jaramiqa—a Persian tribe which had settled near Mosul during the early years of Islam—and by Nabateans. It stood on the edge of the Qatul Canal, which is one of the canals which flows out of the Tigris. He built a palace and soon the people of Baghdad, responding to his summons, emigrated there, leaving the capital almost abandoned. It is to this event that one of the "vagabond" poets refers in the piece in which he reproaches Mu'tasim for his desertion of his subjects, saying:

> Oh you who live in Qatul in the midst of the Jaramiqa,
> You have left none in Baghdad but arrogant noblemen.

Meanwhile, the troops which had followed the Caliph were suffering cruelly from the cold of that place. The earth was hard and made construction work difficult. One of the soldiers in his suite said on this subject:

They told us Qatul would be our winter encampment,
But we count on the intervention of God, our master,
Men make their plans, but each day
God causes some new disaster to take place.

Discouraged by the drawbacks of the place and the difficulties of building there, Mu'tasim left it and, continuing his search, reached Samarra. At this place, there was an old Christian monastery. The Caliph asked one of the monks who lived there what the place was called. He answered:

"Samarra."

"And what does Samarra mean?" went on the Caliph.

"We find it given," said the monk, "in our ancient books and in the traditions of the past, as meaning the city of Shem, the son of Noah."

"What country is it and of which province is it a part?"

"It is of the country of al-Tirhan, to which it belongs."

Mu'tasim examined the countryside carefully. Vast plains unfolded before his eyes. The air was healthy, the soil fertile. Struck by these advantages and the mildness of the climate, he stopped there for three days, which he spent hunting. He noticed that his appetite was stronger and that he ate more than usual, which he did not fail to attribute to the effect of the climate and the soil and water. He liked it. Then, summoning the people from the monastery, he bought their land for 4,000 dinars. He chose a site to build his palace and the foundations were laid. This is the quarter of Samarra, known as Waziriya, and hence the name "Waziri" given to a quality of fig which is superior to any other, thanks to its sweetness, the smoothness of its flesh and the smallness of its seeds. Neither the figs of Syria, nor those of Hulwan can be compared to this kind.

The building began to rise. He had masons, workmen and craftsmen come from every country, and obtained seedlings and young trees from all around. He distributed land to the Turks in different areas and gave them as neighbours soldiers originally from Fergana, Ushrusana and the cities of Khurasan, always bearing in mind the relative geographical positions of their native lands. Ashnas, the Turk, and his companions were given a grant of the area known as Karkh Samarra and some of the men from Fergana were established in the quarters known as al-Umari and al-Jisr—the Bridge.

The plan of the city was laid out. The different estates, quarters and roads were marked. Each trade and each branch of commerce had its separate market. Everyone began to build his house. Things were going up on every side—houses and solidly built palaces. Agriculture flourished and canals leading from the Tigris and other water courses were dug. When people learned that a new capital was being built, they came crowding in, bringing with them every kind of merchandise and the vast quantities of provisions necessary for the existence of men and animals. Life became rich and easy. Equity, justice and prosperity spread through the land.

The Caliph Mu'tasim began the works we have just described in 221 AH/836 AD.

27

Book of Gifts and Rarities
Eleventh Century

This eleventh-century manuscript by an unknown author who lived in the port city of Tinnis in Egypt between ca. 1052 and 1071 came to light in the fifteenth century, when it was translated by Ahmad ibn al-Rashid Ibn al-Zubayr. According to this manuscript, the author witnessed the exchange of gifts between the Fatimid Caliphate and the Byzantines and had conversations with officials of various levels in various countries about gifts and rare goods in Islamic history. He obviously also collected archives and records about these events. This passage is an account by the vizier (prime minister) of the treasures of Harun al-Rashid, the most powerful ruler of the Abbasid Caliphate when he died in 809. In the stories of the Arabian Nights, Caliph Harun al-Rashid was a legendary figure who amassed great wealth by presiding over an empire whose trade routes encompassed much of Africa and Eurasia. What did his treasures consist of, and how did they reflect the geographic extent of the Abbasid Caliphate?

Ibn al-Zubayr, *Kitab al-Dhakha'ir wa'l-Tuhaf*, trans. Ghada al-Hijjawi al-Qaddumi, as *Book of Gifts and Rarities* (Cambridge, Mass.: Harvard University Press, 1996), 207–8.

Al-Faḍl b. al-Rabi[1] says,

When, in the year 193 [809], al-Amīn assumed the caliphate in succession to his father Harun al-Rashid, he ordered me to count the contents of the treasuries with respect to clothing, furnishings, vessels, and equipment. I brought in the scribes and the treasury keepers and kept on counting for four months. I had never imagined that the treasuries of the caliphate could contain all the things I oversaw [there]! Then I ordered them to write a statement for each category. The treasuries contained [the following articles]:

Four thousand long outer garments [with open front and wide sleeves] made of richly colored fabric; four thousand long outer garments [with open front and long sleeves] made of pure silk lined with sable fur, desert-fox fur, and other kinds of soft hair; ten thousand knee-length closed shirts [with round opening and ample sleeves], along with undergarments; ten thousand long [wide closed] garments; two thousand drawers made of all types of fabric; four thousand turbans; one thousand hooded mantles [worn over the shoulders]; one thousand wraps [not cut or sewn] in various fabrics; five thousand kerchiefs of various kinds; five hundred velvet garments; one hundred thousand *mithqals*[2] of musk; one hundred thousand *mithqals* of ambergris; one thousand baskets of Indian aloeswood; one thousand vessels of baked clay full of costly [strong mixed] scents; many kinds of perfume; precious stones that were valued by the jewelers at four million five hundred thousand dinars;[3] one thousand rings [set with] precious stones; one thousand Armenian carpets; four thousand curtains; five thousand cushions; five thousand pillows; fifteen hundred pile-rugs of pure silk; 100 decorative [pure silk rugs to be placed over] carpets; one thousand cushions and pillows of pure silk; 300 Maysan carpets; one thousand Darabjirdi carpets; one thousand brocade cushions; one thousand cushions of striped pure silk; one thousand pure silk curtains; three hundred brocade curtains; five hundred Tabari carpets; one thousand Tabari cushions; one thousand small arm bolsters; one thousand pillows; one thousand basins [of metal]; one thousand ewers; three hundred braziers; one thousand candlesticks [or candelabra]; two thousand [metalwork] articles in all types of bronze; one thousand [gold or silver] girdles; ten thousand adorned swords; fifty thousand swords for the Shakiriyyah[4]

---

[1] Al-Fadl b. al-Rabi (755–824), chamberlain of Caliph Harun al-Rashid before becoming his vizier, or chief minister. [Translator's note.]

[2] A weight that varied from country to country, but in the range of 4.3–4.7 grams.

[3] Gold coins, each about 4.2 grams, the currency of the Abbasids.

[4] Bodyguards.

and the slave soldiers; one hundred fifty thousand spears; one hundred thousand bows; one thousand [pieces of] special plate armor; fifty thousand [pieces of] ordinary plate armor; ten thousand [egg-shaped] helmets; twenty thousand coats of mail; one hundred fifty thousand shields; four thousand special saddles; 30,000 ordinary saddles; four thousand pairs of high boots, most of them lined with sable and desert fox fur, or other kinds of fur. Inside each boot there was a knife and kerchief; four thousand pairs of socks; four thousand [ceremonial] tents with their equipment; and one hundred fifty thousand camping tents.

8

Trade Networks from the Mediterranean to the South China Sea, Tenth–Thirteenth Centuries

28

CAPTAIN BUZURG IBN SHAHRIYAR

The Book of the Wonders of India

953

Captain Buzurg Ibn Shahriyar from Ramhormuz, in the Persian province of Khuzistan, was a shipmaster who lived in the port of Siraf on the Persian Gulf and collected "yarns"—the stories sailors spread from port to port when they gathered in inns near the harbor where their ships were anchored. This story from his collection tells of a Jewish trader called Ishaq who made a fortune while trading in China and India but aroused much jealousy in merchant circles, which almost cost him his life. It reveals the goods, the profits, and the rivalries among the merchants in the Indian Ocean trade. How did Arabs and Jews cooperate and compete in the Indian Ocean trade?

Among curious stories about seafaring merchants, travellers and men who have made their fortunes at sea, is that of Ishaq b. Yahuda.[1] He

---

[1] His name, the biblical Isaac, is pronounced in Arabic in two syllables as Is-haq. [Translator's note.]

Captain Buzurg Ibn Shahriyar, *The Book of the Wonders of India*, ed. and trans. G. S. P. Freeman-Grenville (London and the Hague: East-West Publications, 1981), 2–64.

152

was a man who earned his living among brokers in Oman. Following a dispute with a Jew, he left Oman and went to India. He had no more than about 200 dinars. After thirty years, during which no one had news of him, he came back to Oman in 300/912. I learnt from several of my seafaring friends that he came from China on a ship that was his own, with all it contained. To avoid customs and the tax of one-tenth, he made an arrangement with the ruler of Oman, Ahmad b. Hilal, for more than one million dirhams. On a single occasion, he sold Ahmad b. Marwan 100,000 mithqals[2] of musk of top quality. The purchaser reckoned it was all he had. He sold the same man 40,000 dinars[3] worth of material, and then did a 20,000 dinar deal with another man. At Ahmad b. Marwan's request, Ishaq agreed to a discount of a silver dirham[4] per mithqal, and this amounted to 100,000 dirhams.

His enormous fortune was the talk of the country, and aroused jealousy. An evil man, who had not been able to get out of Ishaq what he wanted, went to Baghdad to see the vizier, Ali b. Muhammad b. Furat. He did all he could to ruin the Jew's reputation, but the vizier paid no attention. Then the man wormed his way into the confidence of an evil man at the court of [the Caliph] al-Muqtadir-billah. He pretended to give him information, and gave him his own account of the Jew's history. The man, said he, had left Oman without anything, and had come back with a ship loaded with musk worth a million dinars, and silk and porcelain worth the same, and an equal amount in jewels and stones, as well as many rarities from China of incalculable value. He was a childless old man, he added. Ahmad b. Hilal had received 500,000 dinars worth of goods from him.

All this was told to al-Muqtadir, who found it very surprising, and immediately sent one of his black eunuchs, called Fulful,[5] with thirty servants, bearing a message for Ahmad b. Hilal in Oman, ordering him to hand over the Jew to the eunuch, and to send him to himself. When the eunuch got to Oman, and Ahmad b. Hilal learnt the Caliph's orders, he had the Jew arrested, but at the same time promised to get him out of the affair for a substantial sum that he asked for himself. Then he let the merchants know secretly that the Jew's arrest was prejudicial to them, to all foreigners, and to all local business men, if they were to be at the

---

[2] A weight that varied from country to country, but in the range of 4.3–4.7 grams.
[3] Gold coins, each about 4.2 grams, the currency of the Abbasids.
[4] Silver coins, each about 2.7 grams, the currency of the Abbasids.
[5] This is a nickname, Pepper. [Translator's note.]

whim of arbitrary power and the jealousy of the poor and the wicked. Thereon the markets shut. The townsfolk and foreigners signed petitions, complaining that, after the Jew's arrest, vessels would no longer land in Oman, that merchants would leave, that they would advise one another not to frequent the coasts of Iraq, and that there was no longer any security for property. Oman, they added, was a town where there were many very wealthy merchants, but that they had no other guarantee of their security than the justice of the Commander of the Faithful and his Amir, their solicitude for merchants, and their protection against envious and wicked men.

The merchants rioted in the town, crying out against Ahmad b. Hilal. They revolted, so much that the eunuch Fulful and his companions got ready to go and make their farewells. Ahmad b. Hilal wrote to the Caliph, describing what had happened, how the merchants had drawn up their vessels at the quays, and were reloading them to carry their goods away, and that resident business men were upset, saying:

We shall be deprived of our living when ships no longer come here, because Oman is a town where men get everything from the sea. If small men among us are treated like this, it will be worse for the great. Sultans are like a fire that devours everything it touches. We cannot resist it, and it is much better to go away.

The eunuch and his men took 2,000 dinars from the Jew and went away. The Jew was outraged, and made haste to get together all he possessed. He fitted out a ship, and went back to China without leaving a single dirham behind in Oman. At Sarira the ruler asked him for 20,000 dinars transit dues, to let him carry on with his voyage to China. The Jew declined to give anything. The ruler sent men to assassinate him by night, and took his ship and all his property.

Ishaq had lived for three years in Oman. Men who saw him have told me personally that they had seen a black porcelain vase that he had given Ahmad b. Hilal as a present. It had a cover that sparkled like gold.

What is in that vase? Asked Ahmad.

A dish of *sikbaj* [?] that I cooked for you in China, said the Jew.

Sikbaj cooked in China! Two years ago! It must be in a fine state.

He took the cover off the vase, and there were golden fish with ruby eyes, surrounded by musk of the first quality. The contents of the vase were worth 50,000 dinars.

29

Inscription on a Cliff in the Port of Quanzhou

1183

During the Song dynasty (960–1279) and the Yuan dynasty (1279–1368), Quanzhou was the most important port for China's international trade. Local government officials were responsible for protecting commercial vessels coming in and going out of the port. One of their tasks was to perform the annual ritual that called for winds favorable for sailing. The following is a record of one such ritual inscribed on a cliff overlooking the harbor. How did the ritual of calling winds benefit Song China's overseas trade?

In the tenth year of the Chunxi era, the year of Zhaoyan Danyu, the year of Guimao,[1] on the twenty-fourth day of the leap month, Sima Juntong the governor, Zhao Zitao the officer of rites, Lin Shao the customs officer, and Han Jun the military commander, for the purpose of calling the winds to ensure safe sailings of the ships, arrived at Yanfusi Monastery. At the shrine of the "King of Reaching Faraway Lands and Bringing Profit and Welfare to a Vast Population," the rituals were performed. Afterward, while waiting for the tides to change so that they could return home, they visited all the scenic spots and took a brief rest in the Hall of Huaigutang.[2]

[1] The author of the inscription uses three calendrical ways to mark the year, which is 1183.

[2] The hall in memory of ancient times.

Photographed and translated by Xinru Liu.

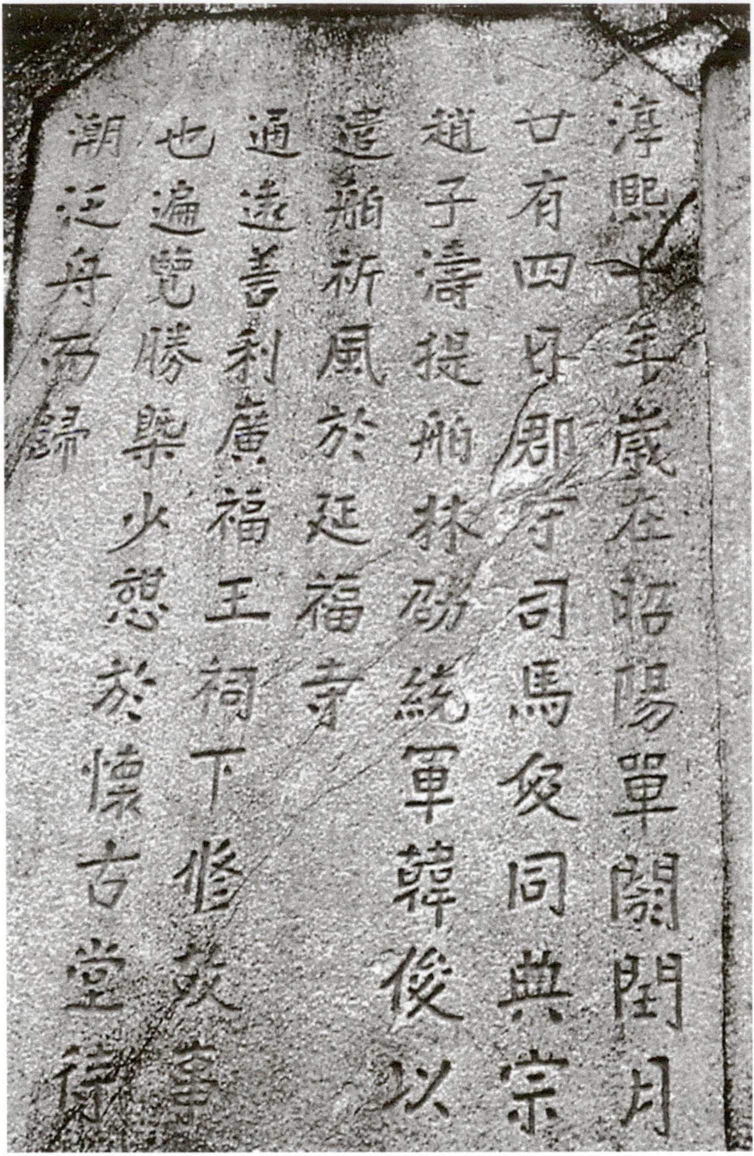

淳熙十年歲在昭陽單閼閏月
廿有四日郡守司馬伋同典崇
趙子濤提舶林硋統軍韓俊以
遣舶祈風於延福寺
通遠善利廣福王祠下修祀事
也遍覽勝槩火恖於懷古堂待
潮汎舟而歸

Figure 4. *Inscription on a Cliff in the Port of Quanzhou, 1183*

30

IBN JUBAYR

The Travels of Ibn Jubayr
ca. 1185

Ibn Jubayr (1145–1217), a Muslim scholar born in Valencia, Spain, was a secretary to the governor of the Islamic Moorish kingdom of Grenada. In 1183 he began a pilgrimage to Mecca and traveled for two years, reaching Baghdad as well as many cities on or near the Mediterranean coast, including the Latin kingdom of Jerusalem. In this passage from his journal of his travels, he observes that the hostilities between the Christian Crusaders of Western Europe and the Muslim powers in the Holy Lands did not inhibit trade. Why did the Crusaders and Muslim rulers let traders cross the borders to trade?

Any stranger in these parts whom God has rendered fit for solitude may, if he wishes, attach himself to a farm and live there the pleasantest life with the most contented mind. Bread in plenty will be given to him by the people of the farm, and he may engage himself in the duties of an imam[1] or in teaching, or what he will, and when he is wearied of the place, he may remove to another farm, or climb Mount Lebanon or Mount Judi and there find the saintly hermits who nothing seek but to please Great and Glorious God, and remain with them so long as he wishes, and then go where he wills. It is strange how the Christians round Mount Lebanon, when they see any Muslim hermits, bring them food and treat them kindly, saying that these men are dedicated to Great and Glorious God and that they should therefore share with them. This mountain is one of the most fertile in the world, having all kinds of fruits, running waters, and ample shade, and rarely is it without a hermit or an ascetic. And if the Christians treat the opponents of their religion in this fashion, what think you of the treatment that the Muslims give each other?

[1] A Muslim leader for prayer, or an authority on scholarship.

Ibn Jubayr, *The Travels of Ibn Jubayr, 1183–1185*, trans. R. J. C. Broadhurst (London: Jonathan Cape, 1952), 300–301.

One of the astonishing things that is talked of is that though the fires of discord burn between the two parties, Muslim and Christian, two armies of them may meet and dispose themselves in battle array, and yet Muslim and Christian travellers will come and go between them without interference. In this connection we saw at this time, that is the month of Jumada 'l-Ula, the departure of Saladin[2] with all the Muslims troops to lay siege to the fortress of Kerak, one of the greatest of the Christian strongholds lying astride the Hejaz road and hindering the overland passage of the Muslims. Between it and Jerusalem lies a day's journey or a little more. It occupies the choicest part of the land in Palestine, and has a very wide dominion with continuous settlements, it being said that the number of villages reaches four hundred. This Sultan invested it, and put it to sore straits, and long the siege lasted, but still the caravans passed successively from Egypt to Damascus, going through the lands of the Franks without impediment from them. In the same way the Muslims continuously journeyed from Damascus to Acre (through Frankish territory), and likewise not one of the Christian merchants was stopped or hindered (in Muslim territories).

The Christians impose a tax on the Muslims in their land which gives them full security; and likewise the Christian merchants pay a tax upon their goods in Muslim lands. Agreement exists between them, and there is equal treatment in all cases. The soldiers engage themselves in their war, while the people are at peace and the world goes to him who conquers. Such is the usage in war of the people of these lands; and in the dispute existing between the Muslim Emirs and their kings it is the same, the subjects and the merchants interfering not. Security never leaves them in any circumstance, neither in peace nor in war. The state of these countries in this regard is truly more astonishing than our story can fully convey. May God by His favour exalt the word of Islam.

---

[2] Saladin (1137?–1193) was a Muslim warrior, the great opponent of the Crusaders.

31

Letter from a Jewish Trader in India to His Wife in Cairo
1204

This personal letter reveals the tensions and misunderstandings that could arise in families long separated by the necessities of foreign trade. The translator observes that "the letter was not sent, but reached Fustat nonetheless, which can only mean that the writer succeeded in coming home. I do not believe that he would have returned to Fustat had his wife accepted the repudiation. He then would have stayed in Aden and married there. Thus the long years of suffering had not been in vain. The India traveler was finally united with his wife." The letter also reveals financial arrangements and relationships among traders and within a trading family. How did the Indian Ocean trade impact Jewish traders' family life?

Escape of the Family from the Plague

Would I try to describe the extent of my feelings of longing and yearning for you all the time, my letter would become too long and the words too many. But He who knows the secrets of the heart has the might to bring about relief for each of us by uniting us in joy.

Your precious letters have arrived; I have read and scrutinized them, and was happy to learn from them that you are well and healthy and that you have escaped from those great terrors, the like of which have not been experienced for many generations.[1] Praise be to God for your deliverance and for granting you respite until you might be recompensed in a measure commensurate with your sufferings.

---

[1] There were both famine and plague in Egypt in 1202–1203. This letter is dated 1204.

Letters of Medieval Jewish Traders, trans. and ed. S. D. Goitein (Princeton, N.J.: Princeton University Press, 1973), 220–26.

The Dedicated Husband

In your letters you alternately rebuke and offend me or put me to shame and use harsh words all the time.[2] I have not deserved any of this. I swear by God, I do not believe that the heart of anyone traveling away from his wife has remained like mine, all the time and during all the years—from the moment of our separation to the very hour of writing this letter—so constantly thinking of you and yearning after you and regretting to be unable to provide you with what I so much desire: your legal rights on every Sabbath[3] and holiday, and to fulfill all your wishes, great and small, with regard to dresses or food or anything else. And you write about me as if I had forgotten you and would not remember you had it not been for your rebukes, and as if, had you not warned me that the public would reprove me, I would not have thought of you. Put this out of your mind and do not impute such things to me. And if what you think or say about my dedication to you is the product of your mind, believing that words of rebuke will increase my yearning—no, in such a way God will not let me reach the fulfillment of my hope, although in my heart there is twice as much as I am able to write. But he is able to have us both reach compensation for our sufferings and then, when we shall be saved, we shall remember in what situation we are now.

Travel beyond the Coromandel Coast

You rebuke me with regard to the ambergris.[4] You poor ones!!! Had you known how much trouble and expenses I have incurred to get this ambergris for you, you would have said: there is nothing like it in the world. This is the story: After I was resurrected from the dead and had lost all that I carried with me I took a loan of [. . .] dinars and traveled

---

[2] This seems to show that the letters had been written by the trader's wife herself. In a letter dictated to a clerk or a relative she would not have gone to such length. [Translator's note.]

[3] A Jewish scholar is bound by law to visit his wife once a week, namely on the night of the Sabbath, that is, Friday night (Talmud Bab. Ketubot 62b). For other occupations other rules are set, but our Indian trader and his wife clearly regarded themselves as belonging to the learned class. [Translator's note.]

[4] A highly valued perfume and medicine, one variety coming from the Indian Ocean and one from the Atlantic. The wife was not satisfied with the quality or quantity of the ambergris sent. [Translator's note.]

to countries beyond al-Ma'bar.[5] I checked my accounts[6] and found [?] with "the decimals."[7] I took them and paid to one of our coreligionists who traveled back from al-Ma'bar to Aden ... ... and for it he bought for you ... [Three lines and the beginning of the words written in the margin damaged.]

Drunk But Pious

This was my way of life from the moment I left you until I arrived in Aden (and from there to India) and from India back to Aden:[8] Day and night I was constantly drinking, not of my free will,[9] but I conducted myself in an exemplary way[10] and if anyone poked fun in foul speech in my presence, I became furious with him, until he became silent, he and others. I constantly fulfilled what God knows, and cured my soul by fasting during the days and praying during the nights. The congregations in Aden and in India often asked me to lead them in prayer, and I am regarded by them and regard myself as a pious man.

[*Here begins the reverse side; the twenty-four first lines are damaged beyond repair. Madmun, meaning no doubt Madmun b. David the trustee of the merchants in Aden, and a shipment of clove are mentioned.* — Translator's note]

As to Divorce—The Choice Is Left to the Wife

Now in one of your letters you adjure me to set you free, then letters arrived from the old man[11] saying the same. Later Ma'ani ["Eloquent"] b. al-Dajaji ["Seller of Fowl"] met me and told me that you came to his house before he set out on his travel. You had given him nutmeg paste as a collateral on a loan of 100 dirhems, but he released 20 dirhems to

---

[5] This is the Coromandel coast of southeastern India. Very few of the thousand or so Jewish India travelers mentioned in the Geniza went as far as the Coromandel coast, but beyond it next to none. Our traveler had to take this exceptional trouble in order to replace his losses. [Translator's note].

[6] An Arab proverb says: "When a Jew is broke, he checks his grandfather's old accounts," meaning that he always finds someone owing him something. This seems to be the situation alluded to here. [Translator's note.]

[7] Arabic *deqat*. A counting machine, it seems, derived from Greek *deka*, ten. [Translator's note.]

[8] It seems that our letter was written there. [Translator's note.]

[9] But because of the grief over the separation from his beloved wife. [Translator's note.]

[10] No slave girls or whores. [Translator's note.]

[11] Her late father. [Translator's note.]

you. Please let me know whether this is correct, in which case I shall return this sum to him. He reported also that you had asked him to return to you letters which your late father — may God have mercy on him — had sent with him, but he had said to you: "I have already packed them away on the boat."[12] Then you said that these letters were not written with your consent and you asked him not to deliver them to me. On this Ma'ani had replied: The judge might have meanwhile sent a message demanding something from the elder,[13] in which case the delivery of these letters might be useful to him.

Now, if this[14] is your wish, I cannot blame you. For the waiting has been long. And I do not know whether the Creator will grant relief immediately so that I can come home, or whether matters will take time, for I cannot come home with nothing. Therefore I resolved to issue a writ which sets you free.[15] Now the matter is in your hand. If you wish separation from me, accept *the bill of repudiation* and you are free. But if this is not your decision and not your desire, do not lose these long years of waiting: perhaps relief is at hand and you will regret at a time when regret will be of no avail.

And please do not blame me, for I never neglected you from the time when those things happened and made an effort to save you and me from people talking and impairing my honor. The refusal[16] was on your side, not on mine. I do not know whether this[17] is your decision or that of someone else, but after all this, please do not say, you or someone else: this[18] is our reward from him and recompense. All day long I have a lonely heart and am pained by our separation. I feel that pain while writing these lines. But the choice is with you; the decision is in your hand: if you wish to carry the matter through, do so; if you wish to leave things as they are, do so. But do not act after the first impulse. Ask the advice of good people and act as you think will be the best for you. May God inspire you with the right decision.

---

[12] From Cairo-Fustat up to Qus one traveled on the Nile. [Translator's note.]

[13] The writer of our letter. [Translator's note.]

[14] Meaning a divorce. [Translator's note.]

[15] A conditional bill of repudiation, which becomes valid as soon as she agrees. [Translator's note.]

[16] To accept a divorce offered by him before when his absence from home became too protracted. [Translator's note.]

[17] Demanding a divorce. [Translator's note.]

[18] The dispatch of the conditional bill of repudiation. [Translator's note.]

Greetings, Errands, Gifts

[*The concluding part is very much damaged. It began in the margin, much of which is lost, continued in the main part of the page and returned to the margin, but was never completed. Clearly the letter was not dispatched; see also the introduction. Only continuous sentences are translated.* — Translator's note]

[Best regards to my sister] and her husband, the illustrious elder Abu 'l-Fada'il, the scholar, to Ma'ani, the scholar [?], and his son. I have exerted myself for him to a degree that only God knows. The elder Abu 'l-Khayr ["Mr. Good"] agreed to pay him 10 mithqals [Egyptian dinars], which the elder Abu 'l-Makarim ["Noble Character"] will deliver to him.[19]

Convey my greetings to the elder Abu Ishaq, the son of your paternal uncle, to his mother, to the elder Abu 'Imran and his children, to [. . .] j, the daughter of your paternal uncle, and to all those whom you know, my most sincere regards.

I sent you 7½ mann of nutmeg, which is better than anything found in the Karim[20] and worth more than other sorts of it by 1 dinar; 11 mann of good galingale;[21] two futa cloths for the children; 2½ of celandine and 25 of odoriferous wood; fourteen pieces in number.[22]

---

[19] Probably a case of inheritance of a merchant who had died in Aden. Abu 'l-Khayr was in Aden and Abu 'l-Makarim in Cairo-Fustat. [Translator's note.]

[20] The goods going from India to the West. [Translator's note.]

[21] Arabic *khawlanj*, from which the English word is derived; a plant from the ginger family serving as an aphrodisiac or as a constituent in narcotics. [Translator's note.]

[22] These quantities of costly Oriental products were not really "gifts," but destined to be sold and to serve for the upkeep of the family. [Translator's note.]

32

ZHAO RUKUO

Records concerning Foreign Countries

1225

Zhao Rukuo (1170–1231) wrote a book about foreign countries when he was the administrator of overseas trade for Fujian Province. Quanzhou, the most important port in the province, was under his direct supervision, and there he gathered information from both Chinese and foreign traders and sailors. In this passage he writes about Hainan, China's second largest island and the southern frontier of its imperial power since the Han dynasty. The island supplied tropical goods to the Chinese mainland. People sailing from Hainan to Quanzhou used the compass to guide them. The compass had been invented in China many centuries before for use in locating auspicious sites for residences and burials. By the thirteenth century, it was also used to guide navigation on the long and complicated voyages of international trade. In this account, notice the local products that had now entered the international market.

During Han times Hainan was called Zhuya and Dan'er. During the military campaign in the southern Yue region, Emperor Wudi of the Han sent an expedition that left from Xuwen Peninsula and crossed the strait in order to occupy the island. . . . From the fifth year of the Zhenyuan era[1] to the present, Qiong has been the headquarters of the local government.

A port called Dijiaochang on the Xuwen Peninsula[2] faces Qiong on Hainan, which lies about 360 *li*[3] across the sea. It takes half a day to sail across the strait with a good wind. A location called Sanheliu[4] in the middle of the route is so dangerous that the sailors raise their hands to

[1] 789.
[2] On the mainland.
[3] About one hundred miles.
[4] Literally, the meeting of three currents.

Zhao Rukuo, *Zhu Fan Zhi* [Records concerning Foreign Countries], ed. Yang Bowen (Beijing: Zhonghua Shuju, 2000), 216. Translated by Xinru Liu.

congratulate each other if they do not run into any storms. After reaching Jiyang, one realizes that one is on the [Southern] Ocean, and there are no more landmarks to guide the way. In the ocean there are islands called Wuli, Sumi, and Jilang. Looking farther south, there is Champa;[5] toward the west there is Zhenla;[6] and toward the east there are vast coral reefs.[7] Sailing on the ocean one sees no horizon, since the colors of the sky and the water merge together. The ships that come and go on the ocean have no means of guidance except for the directions given by the needle of the compass. Sailors watch the compass day and night without pause, since the smallest negligence could cost them their lives.

The four prefectures with eleven counties under them are subject to the administration of the Western Circuit of Guangnan. The administrative regions circle around Limu Mountain, where the barbarian Li people dwell. Some Li people are savages, and some are more civilized. Many parts of their land are not claimed, and the limited rice crops are not enough to feed the population. In order to get more food to feed themselves, they plant much taro and other cereal for making porridge. Therefore it is common for the people to trade all kinds of fragrant materials to make a living. Local products include:

Fragrance wood from agallocha[8]
Fragrance made from *Penglai* [?]
Fragrance made from *Zheguban* [?]
Zhanxiang[9]
Shengxiang[10]
Clover
Areca or betel nut
Coconut
Kapok, or tree cotton
Ramie
Paper made with mulberry bark
Red and white rattan
Multicolored rough cloth
Lemons
Dark cassia wood

[5] The central and southern areas of modern Vietnam.
[6] Cambodia.
[7] The modern Xisha and Nansha archipelagos in the South China Sea.
[8] *Chenxiang* in the Chinese record.
[9] A lower quality of *chenxiang*.
[10] Another variety of *chenxiang*.

Huali wood[11]
Oil of sea plum [?]
Agar plant[12]
Sea lacquer [?]
Pepper
Galangal[13]
Fish air bladder
Yellow wax
Stone crab
Etc.

All these goods are obtained from the communities of the Li people. Other people who live nearby buy these items from the Li with salt, iron, fish, and rice, and then trade these regional goods to the [long-distance] traders who come into their ports. Merchant ships from Quanzhou carry liquor, rice, wheat flour, gauze silk, lacquerware, porcelain ware, and so forth to Hainan in order to trade for the tropical goods there. These ships depart China at the end of the year or during the first month of the new year, and return around the fifth or sixth month of the year. If a ship has loaded fresh betel nuts, it sails back north before the others in order to arrive in the fourth month of the year.

[11] *Dalbergia hainanensis*, a fragrant wood.
[12] A marine algae.
[13] A tropical ginger, one of the products the Jewish trader traveled to southern India to obtain. See Document 31, note 21.

33

MARCO POLO

The Travels of Marco Polo, the Venetian

ca. 1298

Marco Polo (ca. 1254–1324) is famous in modern times, but when stories of his travels from Venice to the court of Khubilai Khan in China were recorded and compiled into a book by Rusticello of Pisa, a fellow prisoner in Genoese captivity, no one took him seriously. Some of

Marco Polo, *The Travels of Marco Polo, the Venetian*, trans. W. Marsden, rev. and ed. Thomas Wright, Esq. (London: Henry G. Bohn, 1854), 336–37.

Polo's descriptions, such as burning a "black stone" for fuel, were simply unimaginable to thirteenth-century Europeans, even well-traveled Italians. By the fifteenth century, however, The Travels of Marco Polo *was one of the first books printed in Europe and was immensely influential. All the great adventurers, including Christopher Columbus and Vasco da Gama, read it and carried a copy on their voyages. Marco Polo was a shrewd merchant and keen observer of commodities and markets. Everywhere he traveled he paid attention to government regulations and taxes. The following passage is his observation of tax collection in a large city of the Mongol Empire. Marco Polo had a hard time convincing his country people at that time what he had told about China was true. Do you believe what he said here?*

Of the Revenues of the Grand Khan

We shall now speak of the revenue which the grand khan draws from the city of Kin-sai[1] and the places within its jurisdiction, constituting the ninth division or kingdom of Mauji. In the first place, upon salt, the most productive article, he levies a yearly duty of eighty tomans of gold, each toman being eighty thousand saggi, and each saggio fully equal to a gold florin, and consequently amounting to six millions four hundred thousand ducats.[2] This vast produce is occasioned by the vicinity of the province to the sea, and the number of salt lakes or marshes, in which, during the heat of summer, the water becomes crystallized, and from whence a quantity of salt is taken, sufficient for the supply of five of the other divisions of the province. There is here cultivated and manufactured a large quantity of sugar, which pays, as do all other groceries, three and one-third per cent. The same is also levied upon the wine, or fermented liquor, made of rice. The twelve classes of artisans, of whom we have already spoken, as having each a thousand shops, and also the merchants, as well those who import the goods into the city, in the first instance, as those who carry them from thence to the interior, or who export them by sea, pay, in like manner, a duty of three and one-third per cent.; but goods coming by sea from distant countries and regions, such as from India, pay ten per cent. So likewise all native articles of the

---

[1] Chinese Xingzai, another name for Hangzhou or Lin'an, the capital of the Southern Song dynasty. It was part of the Mongol Empire when Marco Polo visited there, and the Mongol government collected large revenues by taxing both agriculture and trade.

[2] One Venetian *saggio* (plural *saggi*) weighed a sixth of a British ounce. A ducat was a gold coin widely used in Europe. [Translator's note.]

country, as cattle, the vegetable produce of the soil, and silk, pay a tithe to the king. The account being made up in the presence of Marco Polo, he had an opportunity of seeing that the revenue of his majesty, exclusively of that arising from salt, already stated, amounted in the year to the sum of two hundred and ten tomans (each toman being eighty thousand saggi of gold), or sixteen million eight hundred thousand ducats.

34

SONG LIAN AND OTHERS

History of the Yuan Dynasty

1370

Song Lian (1310–1381) was a famous scholar in the imperial academy of the Ming dynasty (1368–1644) who was in charge of compiling the official history of the previous Yuan dynasty. He led a group of scholars in selecting significant documents from the archives left by the Mongol court and produced the book in just three years. This history records that after the Mongol regime established its capital in Dadu (modern Beijing), Khubilai declared himself emperor of the Yuan dynasty of China (1271). He soon became interested in gaining control of the flourishing maritime trade along China's southeastern coast. Ever since Genghis Khan's reign, Mongol rulers had been employing Muslim traders to bring precious goods east to their courts by way of overland routes. Khubilai now expanded the flow of goods by using experienced Muslim traders already based in Quanzhou, the major seaport on China's southeastern coast. Thereafter they carried out Mongol trade on the vast overseas networks of Southeast Asia. The following passage from the official history records a decree issued in 1278 by Khubilai welcoming foreign traders and travelers. Why did Khubilai send Muslim traders as his envoys to Southeast Asian countries?

Song Lian and Others, *Yuan Shi* [History of the Yuan Dynasty] (Beijing: Zhonghua Shuju, 1976), 10: 204. Translated by Xinru Liu.

In the fifteenth year of the Zhiyuan era[1] . . . his majesty summoned Suodu, Pu Shougeng,[2] and other officials in [Jiangzhe] Province and issued the following order:

Among the numerous countries located on the islands that are southeast of us, there are many people who admire my country. You may send my message to these people by giving it to travelers on foreign ships. Whenever they come to this land to offer us tribute, I will be their patron. They may come and go and carry out their business as they like.

[1] 1278.
[2] An eminent Muslim trader in Quanzhou. He welcomed the Mongol army's takeover of the city and agreed to serve the Mongol regime.

A Chronology of the Silk Roads
(Second Century BCE–Thirteenth Century CE)

753 BCE–476 CE   From its legendary founding in 753 BCE, Rome expands into an empire that encompasses the Mediterranean world.

Sixth–first centuries BCE   Greek city-states emerge, colonize the Mediterranean, and give way to the rise of Rome.

334–323 BCE   Alexander the Great of Macedonia leads military expeditions as far east as India.

Mid-third century BCE   Bactria and Sogdiana are Hellenized by settlements of Greek soldiers.

Ca. 250 BCE–226 CE   The Parthian Empire rules Persia (modern Iran).

221–206 BCE   The Qin dynasty unites China, extends the Great Wall, and initiates the trade in Chinese silk for horses with nomadic peoples.

206 BCE–220 CE   The Han dynasty rules China and expands the silk–horse trade.

Second century BCE–second century CE   Petra flourishes as a caravan city.

140–87 BCE   Han emperor Wudi settles soldiers along the Great Wall and in the Western Regions, and these farming settlements grow into oasis towns along what will be the Silk Roads.

Late second century BCE   The Yuezhi, migrating west, arrive in Bactria, settling the agricultural land and its Hellenistic cities and eventually establishing the Kushan regime.

129 BCE   Zhang Qian reaches the court of the Yuezhi on the banks of the Oxus River in Bactria and leaves a year later to return to China with reports of the "heavenly horses" of the Western Regions.

Ca. 50 CE   The Kushans cross the Hindu Kush to enter India, establishing an empire across Central and South Asia.

First century CE Buddhism starts to spread out of India via Afghanistan.

First–second centuries CE Parthia and India trade with the Romans "at sea," that is, through the ports of the Persian Gulf and western India.

224–651 CE The Sassanid Empire rules Persia.

Late third century CE Buddhism takes hold in Central Asia and China.

Late third–early fourth centuries Kharoshthi script is used in Niya, evidence of linguistic transmission along the Silk Roads.

Fourth–fifth centuries The Bamiyan Buddhist complex develops.

313 Emperor Constantine's edict of toleration allows Christianity to be practiced in the Roman Empire.

366 The Mogao caves in Dunhuang are established.

386–534 The Xianbei conquer other petty states of nomadic origin and establish the Northern Wei dynasty, which rules China until 534.

395–1453 The Byzantine Empire rules in the eastern Mediterranean and for a while controls the production and consumption of silk textiles.

460 The Northern Wei emperor starts to have huge statues of the Buddha carved at Yungang.

589–618 The Sui dynasty unifies China and rules until 618.

Seventh century Turkic tribes, originally from Mongolia, migrate to Central Asia and begin conquests that replace Indo-European languages with Turkish languages.

618–907 The Tang dynasty rules China and acts as the great patron of the Silk Roads.

638 Christian missionaries travel to China and establish a church in Chang'an.

651 Muslim Arabs conquer Persia and begin the spread of Islam.

661–750 The Umayyad Caliphate establishes the first Islamic empire based in Damascus.

705 Arab armies begin the conquest of Central Asia.

750–1258 The Abbasid Caliphate rules from Baghdad.

845 The Tang emperor Wuzong banishes all foreign religions from China.

Ca. 846–1310 The Chola dynasty rules in India.

960–1279 The Song dynasty rules China.

969–1171 The Fatimid Caliphate rules Egypt.

1096–1204   Christian Crusaders fail to take permanent control of the Holy Lands but spur interest in trade and exploration.

Early thirteenth century   The Mongols begin their conquest of Eurasia.

1279–1368   The Yuan dynasty rules China.

Questions for Consideration

1. Describe the origins and the development of the silk trade. Where, why, and how did it begin? Why did it flourish? What goods came to be traded in exchange for silk?

2. What geographical and ecological features made Central Asia a cross-roads of trade and communications as well as a path of migrations and invasions?

3. Describe the content and purpose of court histories, not only the dynastic histories of China but also the histories of empires and emperors by Greek and Roman authors. What do these histories include? What do they leave out?

4. Explain how the archaeological record provides information about daily life in ancient China and along the Silk Roads that court histories do not include.

5. The history of the Silk Roads is also the history of the rise and fall of empires. Describe the various strategies devised by the large agricultural empires for dealing with the nomadic peoples outside their borders. How did they expand their empires and their control? Consider the Han, Tang, and Yuan Chinese dynasties, the empires of Alexander the Great and Rome, and the Kushans.

6. How did imperial strategies for expansion and control relate to Silk Roads trade? Consider the Chinese, the Kushans, the Byzantines, and the Muslim caliphates.

7. Describe the relationship of nomadic peoples to trade along the Silk Roads. What was their relationship to the agricultural empires? What strategies did they use for dealing with and even conquering the agricultural empires?

8. Which religions spread along the Silk Roads? How were they spread? Which were most successful in gaining converts?

9. What impact did the spread of Buddhism, in particular, have on Silk Roads trade? Explain.

10. Which imperial powers insisted on religious conformity, and which were tolerant of various religions? How did religious tolerance affect Silk Roads trade?

11. Compare and contrast the Chinese (various dynasties) and the Roman and the Byzantine attitudes toward trade and the control of trade. Why were imperial monopolies established over silk?

12. As early as the first century CE, during the height of the Roman Empire, some trade with the East went by sea. Describe the land and sea routes that were used and the goods traded in the ports of Arabia and India.

13. Explain why sea routes eventually replaced land routes across Central Asia for the shipment of trade goods.

14. List all the goods that traveled the Silk Roads. Describe the evolution from trade in luxuries to trade in goods that ordinary people could afford, at least some of the time, and came to depend on.

15. What sorts of currencies did people use when trading on the Silk Roads? How did coins facilitate trade, and what evidence do they provide of cultural diffusion?

16. Describe linguistic transmission on the Silk Roads. What is the evidence?

17. How did the rise of Islam and the establishment of Muslim empires affect trade?

18. Describe all the ways, places, and times that silk — especially when dyed purple — signified prestige. What is the relationship between dress and social status? How did rulers exercise control of their subjects through the wearing of silk?

19. Generalize about the travelers on the Silk Roads. Who were they? Why were they traveling? What records did they leave? Assess the impact of travelers' accounts on Silk Roads trade and on our understanding of the Silk Roads today.

20. List all the types of documents that can be used to compile a history of the Silk Roads. What do different types of documents reveal? What do they conceal? How should documents be interpreted? How can cultural artifacts also serve as documents?

Selected Bibliography

Allsen, Thomas. *Commodity and Exchange in the Mongol Empire: A Cultural History of Islamic Textiles.* Cambridge, U.K.: Cambridge University Press, 1997.

This study describes how Mongol rulers deliberately spared skilled artisans and traders during military campaigns so that they could deploy them to the steppe or to remote locations where they made or traded prestigious silk textiles and other commodities.

———. *Culture and Conquest in Mongol Eurasia.* Cambridge, U.K.: Cambridge University Press, 2001.

This book addresses the cultural impact of the Mongol conquests, focusing on communications and exchanges between the Il Khanate in Iran and the Yuan dynasty in China.

Barfield, Thomas. *The Perilous Frontier: Nomadic Empires and China, 221 BC to AD 1757.* Cambridge, Mass.: Blackwell Publishers, 1989.

This analysis of China's northern frontier provides cutting-edge research on the interactions between nomads and sedentary agricultural societies in the ancient world.

Barthold, W. *Turkestan Down to the Mongol Invasion,* 4th English ed., trans. Mrs. T. Minorsky, ed. C. E. Bosworth. Cambridge, U.K.: E. J. W. Gibb Memorial Trust, printed by the University of Cambridge Press, 1977; reprint, 2007.

Barthold combined archaeological and anthropological surveys of Central Asia with literary sources in order to explore multiethnic and multi-linguistic historical streams. This Russian scholar's work is highly valued; during the twentieth century this book, first published in Russian in 1900, was translated into English by several scholars and published in four editions.

Benjamin, Craig G. R. *The Yuezhi: Origin, Migration and the Conquest of Northern Bactria.* Turnhout, Belgium: Brepols Publishers, 2007.

This book provides a comprehensive summary of the available sources on nomadic migrations during the early stage of the Silk Roads. It provides a good base from which to discuss relations between nomads and sedentary populations.

Bowen, R. L., and F. P. Albright. *Archaeological Discoveries in South Arabia*. Baltimore: Johns Hopkins University Press, 1958.

This archaeological report reveals the highly developed settlements and incense industry in ancient southern Arabia.

Bulliet, Richard. *Cotton, Climate, and Camels in Early Islamic Iran: A Moment in World History.* New York: Columbia University Press, 2009.

Bulliet analyzes the "cotton boom" in early Islamic Iran using statistics and factoring in political, economic, and religious changes. The book looks into the *tiraz* system from the perspective of a common textile—cotton—instead of silk, an elite textile.

Cribb, Joe, and Georgina Hermann, eds. *After Alexander: Central Asia before Islam*. New York: Published for the British Academy by Oxford University Press, 2007.

This collection of recent archaeological research on Central Asia focuses on Bactria (the Tukharistan region), in what is now northern Afghanistan, and examines the transition of nomadic peoples into town dwellers engaged in long-distance trade.

Gordon, Stewart, ed. *Robes and Honor: The Medieval World of Investiture*. New York: Palgrave, 2001.

This collection of essays explores the role of prestigious textiles in nation building and the display of a political hierarchy in the medieval world. The demand from the ruling elites helps to explain the flow of prestigious commodities on the Silk Roads.

Hawkes, Jason, and Akira Shimada, eds. *Buddhist Stupas in South Asia*. New Delhi: Oxford University Press, 2009.

This collection of articles addresses the relationship between Buddhism and commercial activities, thereby illuminating the role of Buddhism in the Silk Roads trade.

Hodgson, Marshall G. S. *The Venture of Islam*, vols. 1–2. Chicago: University of Chicago Press, 1974.

These volumes constitute a general history of the Islamic conquests and provide a historical framework for the rise of an Islamic infrastructure along the Silk Roads.

Hopkirk, Peter. *Foreign Devils on the Silk Road*. London: Murray, 1980.

This study of European adventurers and explorers in northwestern China during the late nineteenth and early twentieth centuries explains how the Silk Roads came to the attention of modern academia.

Hourani, George Fadlo. *Arab Seafaring in the Indian Ocean in Ancient and Early Medieval Times*, rev. and expanded by John Carswell. Princeton, N.J.: Princeton University Press, 1995.

This book studies the technology of shipbuilding and navigation by Arab peoples.

Juliano, Annette L., and Judith A. Lerner, eds. *Monks and Merchants: Silk Road Treasures from Northwest China*. New York: Harry N. Abrams, with the Asia Society, 2002.

This is a collection of art history surveys of cave temples and settlements along ancient trade routes in northwestern China. The narrative is accompanied by excellent plates of the religious icons as well as representations of the patrons who sponsored the production of these ancient treasures.

Kennedy, Hugh. *When Baghdad Ruled the Muslim World.* Cambridge, Mass.: Da Capo Press, 2005.

This book provides a cultural history of the Abbasid Caliphate, including a description of the splendid court decoration when the caliph Muqtadir received a delegation from Constantinople in 917.

Khazanov, Anatoly, and Andre Wink, eds. *Nomads in the Sedentary World.* London: Curzon Press, 2001.

This study of nomads and the sedentary world across Eurasia and Africa advances understanding of this issue in world history.

La Vaissière, Étienne de. *Sogdian Traders: A History*, trans. James Ward. Leiden: Brill Academic Publishers, 2005.

Using data from literary and archaeological sources, this study focuses on the organizational structure of Sogdian trading communities and their trading networks along the Silk Roads.

Liu, Xinru. *Ancient India and Ancient China: Trade and Religious Exchanges, AD 1–600.* New Delhi: Oxford University Press, 1988.

This study points out correlations between Buddhist theological developments and commercial activities on the Silk Roads.

————. *Silk and Religion: An Exploration of Material Life and the Thought of People, AD 600–1200.* New Delhi: Oxford University Press, 1996.

This study of material life and religion points out that the theologies and practices of Buddhism, Christianity, and Islam were among the most essential motivations for commerce in the premodern world.

Lopez, R. S. "Silk Industry in the Byzantine Empire." *Speculum* 20 (1945): 1–43.

This article is a comprehensive study on the role of the silk industry in Byzantine diplomacy, defense, and religious life.

Marshak, Boris. *Legends, Tales, and Fables in the Art of Sogdiana.* New York: Bibliotheca Persica Press, 2002.

The author excavated and researched wall paintings at Pendjikent, one of the Sogdian oases, now located in Uzbekistan. His analysis of the artworks reveals religious practices and daily life in the homeland of the Sogdian people.

Marshall, John. *Taxila.* Cambridge, U.K.: Cambridge University Press, 1951.

This study of excavations of urban structures and various utensils in this ancient city (now in Pakistan) reveals cultural transitions during the Persian, Greek, and then Kushan periods of occupation.

Ray, Himanshu. *Monastery and Guild: Commerce under the Satavahanas.* New Delhi: Oxford University Press, 1986.

This study explores the connections between the Roman presence in the Indian trade and the development of Buddhist cave monasteries along the mountainous routes linking western Indian seaports to urban centers in central and northern India.

Rostovtzeff, M. *Caravan Cities*, trans. D. and T. Talbot Rice. Oxford, U.K.: Oxford University Press, 1932; reprint, New York: AMS Press, 1971.

This book surveys the archaeological ruins of caravan cities in the eastern Mediterranean region, from Jordan to Syria and Iraq. It describes the robust trade in various kinds of incense and textiles that the caravans provided.

Sardini, Victor. *The Golden Hoard of Bactria*. New York: Harry N. Abrams; Leningrad: Aurora Art Publishers, 1985.

This is an archaeological report on the excavations of tombs of Kushan kings in Tillya Tepe, Afghanistan.

Schmidt-Colinet, Andreas, Annemarie Stauffer, and Khaled Al-As'ad. *Die Textilien aus Palmyra*. Mainz am Rhein: Verlag Philipp von Zabern, 2000.

This is a catalog of more than five hundred pieces of textiles excavated from the cemetery of Palmyra.

Sen, Tansen. *Buddhism, Diplomacy, and Trade: The Realignment of Sino-Indian Relations, 600–1400*. Honolulu: University of Hawaii Press, 2003.

This book covers religious and commercial activities on the eastern section of the Silk Roads during the Tang and Song dynasties.

Young, Gary K. *Rome's Eastern Trade: International Commerce and Imperial Policy, 31 BC–AD 305*. London and New York: Routledge, 2001.

This study connects the Roman Empire's overseas trade in silk and eastern luxuries to its internal economic interests and imperial agenda.

Acknowledgments (*continued from p. iv*)

Figure 1: Image copyright © The Metropolitan Museum of Art / Art Resource, N.Y.

Figure 2: Vanni / Art Resource, N.Y.

Figure 3: Werner Forman / Art Resource, N.Y.

Document 1: From *Records of the Grand Historian of China, Volume 2*, by Sima Qian, translated by Burton Watson. Copyright © 1961 Columbia University Press. Reprinted with permission of the publisher.

Document 4: Reprinted by permission of the publishers and the Trustees of the Loeb Classical Library from *Strabo: Geography, Volume I*, Loeb Classical Library Volume 211, translated by Horace L. Jones, Cambridge, Mass.: Harvard University Press, Copyright © 1928, by the President and Fellows of Harvard College. Loeb Classical Library ® is a registered trademark of the President and Fellows of Harvard College.

Document 5: *The Campaigns of Alexander, by Arrian*, translated by Aubrey de Sélincourt, Penguin Books, 1971. Used by permission of David Higham Associates.

Document 6: Reprinted by permission of the publishers and the Trustees of the Loeb Classical Library from *Pliny: Natural History, Volume II*, Loeb Classical Library Volume 352, translated by H. Rackham, Cambridge, Mass.: Harvard University Press, Copyright © 1942, by the President and Fellows of Harvard College. Loeb Classical Library ® is a registered trademark of the President and Fellows of Harvard College. Reprinted by permission of the publishers and the Trustees of the Loeb Classical Library from *Pliny: Natural History, Volume IV*, Loeb Classical Library Volume 370, translated by H. Rackham, Cambridge, Mass.: Harvard University Press, Copyright © 1945, by the President and Fellows of Harvard College. Loeb Classical Library ® is a registered trademark of the President and Fellows of Harvard College. Reprinted by permission of the publishers and the Trustees of the Loeb Classical Library from *Pliny: Natural History, Volume III*, Loeb Classical Library Volume 353, translated by H. Rackham, Cambridge, Mass.: Harvard University Press, Copyright © 1940, by the President and Fellows of Harvard College. Loeb Classical Library ® is a registered trademark of the President and Fellows of Harvard College. Reprinted by permission of the publishers and the Trustees of the Loeb Classical Library from *Pliny: Natural History, Volume X*, Loeb Classical Library Volume 419, translated by D. E. Eichholz, Cambridge, Mass.: Harvard University Press, Copyright © 1962, by the President and Fellows of Harvard College. Loeb Classical Library ® is a registered trademark of the President and Fellows of Harvard College.

Document 7: Lionel Casson, *The Periplus Maris Erythraei*. © 1989 Princeton University Press. Reprinted by permission of Princeton University Press.

Document 13: *A Translation of the Kharoshthi Documents from Chinese Turkestan*, by Thomas Burrow, Royal Asiatic Society, 1940. Permission of the Royal Asiatic Society, Great Britain and Ireland.

Document 14: *Monks and Merchants: Silk Road Treasures from Northwest China*, Annette L. Juliano and Judith A. Lerner, translated by Nicholas Sims-Williams © 2001. Published by Harry N. Abrams and The Asia Society.

Document 19: Reprinted by permission of the publishers and the Trustees of the Loeb Classical Library from *Procopius: History of the Wars, Volume V*, Loeb Classical Library Volume 217, translated by H. B. Dewing, Cambridge, Mass.: Harvard University Press, Copyright © 1928, by the President and Fellows of Harvard College. Loeb Classical Library ® is a registered trademark of the President and Fellows of Harvard College. Reprinted by permission of the publishers and the Trustees of the Loeb Classical Library from *Procopius: History of the Wars, Volume I*, Loeb Classical Library Volume 48, translated by H. B. Dewing, Cambridge, Mass.: Harvard University Press, Copyright ©

Index